SCHOOL LIBRARY COLLECTION DEVELOPMENT

**Recent Titles in the Libraries Unlimited
Just the Basic Series**

School Library Spaces: Just the Basics
Written and Illustrated by Patricia A. Messner and Brenda S. Copeland

School Library Management: Just the Basics
Written and Illustrated by Patricia A. Messner and Brenda S. Copeland

SCHOOL LIBRARY COLLECTION DEVELOPMENT

JUST THE BASICS

Claire Gatrell Stephens and Patricia Franklin

Just the Basics

LIBRARIES UNLIMITED

AN IMPRINT OF ABC-CLIO, LLC
Santa Barbara, California • Denver, Colorado • Oxford, England

Library of Congress Cataloging-in-Publication Data

Stephens, Claire Gatrell.
    School library collection development : just the basics / Claire G. Stephens and Patricia Franklin.
        pages cm. — (Just the basics)
    Includes index.
    ISBN 978-1-59884-943-1 (pbk.) — ISBN 978-1-59884-944-8 (e-book) (print)   1. School libraries—Collection development— United States.   2. Collection management (Libraries)—United States. I. Franklin, Patricia, 1951–   II. Title.
    Z675.S3S774   2012
    025.2′1878—dc23   2012016990

ISBN: 978-1-59884-943-1
EISBN: 978-1-59884-944-8

16   15   14   13   12   1   2   3   4   5

This book is also available on the World Wide Web as an eBook.
Visit www.abc-clio.com for details.

Libraries Unlimited
An Imprint of ABC-CLIO, LLC

ABC-CLIO, LLC
130 Cremona Drive, P.O. Box 1911
Santa Barbara, California 93116-1911

This book is printed on acid-free paper ∞

Manufactured in the United States of America

Destiny screen shot (Photo 1.1B) used with permission of Follett Software Company. Copyright © 2011.

Photos 1.3, 1.4, and icons for Top 10 and FAQ © 2011 Jupiterimages Corporation.

CONTENTS

SERIES FOREWORD

School libraries are places to read, to explore, and to find information. When kindergarten students first visit a school library, they are told that this is the place where they will learn answers to their questions and that they will learn how to use the library to find those answers. And, as students grow and mature, the school library does indeed become that place for them, but we know that does not just happen. It takes a community, and that community is the library staff. The library staff must be knowledgeable, hardworking, and service oriented. They must possess a certain amount of basic information just to keep the library up and running.

Basic information is important information. It is often critical and in some cases not readily available. Running a school library well requires the assistance of several key individuals (library aides or clerks, volunteers, paraprofessionals, and technicians), in addition to the professional school librarian. Training these assistants to do the tasks required is time-consuming, and often school librarians and district library coordinators have to construct their own training materials as well as do the one-on-one instruction at each library site.

In order to facilitate and help expedite this training, we offer this series of short, concise, and very practical books to aide in the training necessary to prepare assistants to help: organize, equip, and furnish a media center; manage a school library; prepare and circulate materials; and perform many other tasks that are necessary to the smooth operation of a school library today. The Just The Basics series is written by professionally trained and certified building-level school librarians working currently in the field. As we roll out this series, please let us know what you think. Do we need additional topics? Is the series usable in training situations? What comments do you have?

Please contact me at scoatney@abc-clio.com.

SHARON COATNEY

Senior Acquisitions Editor
Libraries Unlimited
An Imprint of ABC-CLIO, LLC

INTRODUCTION

Working in a school library is one of the most exciting jobs that education has to offer. Where else can you work with children and teachers in a stimulating learning environment and have fun shopping for resources that all of your customers can utilize? The practice of selecting and purchasing library resources is part of the collection development process. Other parts of collection development include removal of outdated materials and tracking and maintaining the collection. Collection development can be time-consuming and complicated. New books and other media are published all the time. There is no way that any one person can read every new book or review each new video or piece of computer software on the market. Technology changes quickly and our students deserve to have information access that keeps them competitive with students around the world. Consider how formats have changed over the last century. Just providing music has been a dilemma. The school libraries maintain equipment to play music, but in what format? First, long-play records (33 RPM) contained the music of choice. Soon music was available on 45s, then cassettes and eight-track tapes. Soon after that compact discs (CDs) took over the market and then MP3 players made downloadable audio files the format of choice. Now students and teachers alike just download what they need from the Internet. Music is at their fingertips. However even with downloadable music, there is cause for stocking audio recordings in the media center collection, but how do you decide what to purchase? The example of music is not unique. Consider this: When buying videos, should we purchase Blu-ray or regular DVDs? What about streaming video services? In all areas—books, magazines, media, software—how do we decide what are priority purchases for our collection?

One of your primary jobs when you are working in the school library is gathering and maintaining materials. With so much to choose from, this can be a daunting task. If you are able to have input on spending funds to purchase what your students and teachers need, ask questions and wisely spend the limited funds available. Those new to the school library typically ask, isn't it easier to just buy 10 copies of the same book than to look for books that are right for our students? If a salesman comes by with a ready-made list, isn't it easier just to buy what he has? Why not duplicate an order created by another school? But your students and teachers are not the same as that other school. And that salesman has no idea what your teachers teach. Getting to know your customers (students, teachers, and parents) and your curriculum will make your job easier and result in a collection that is loved and used. No one wants to see dust gathering on books and equipment that no one uses.

Collection development is a long-term, ongoing process. Those new to working in libraries may think that they can invest time in collection development during their first year and then be done with it. However, school curriculum is always changing and collections must stay aligned with those changes. Each year the library collection development process must begin again in order to improve the library collection to meet the needs of the school community. District librarians know the curriculum changes as they are being made and can help you understand how your collection needs to improve to meet those changes.

District librarians are ready and willing to help you develop a collection that will create a library that your customers will love. When approaching collection development, keep in mind the curriculum and your school community. Again, district librarians as well as teachers at your school can help with this task. Consider the best way to get information to your school community so that they use the resources you gather. In this book, you will find ways to make the job of collection development easier and to make the school library a place where students and teachers alike can find what they need to teach, learn, and grow.

CHAPTER 1
COLLECTION DEVELOPMENT

Anyone working in a school library wears many hats. One of the most important aspects of the job that is often overlooked is collection development. Collection development is the art of selecting, ordering, processing, and maintaining all of the resources that the school library has to offer its patrons. The collection includes print materials, such as books or magazines; and audiovisual materials, such as DVDs and audiobooks on CD or in MP3 format. The collection includes anything that patrons can physically hold and check out of the library, such as equipment or visual aids such as model skeletons, maps, globes, and so forth. The collection also goes beyond the walls of the school. Today, online resources such as e-books, online databases, as well as websites, blogs, or wikis that we find or develop are considered part of the collection. Developing the collection is an ongoing process that can be very time-consuming. It is a job that no one really notices as it is performed, but everyone always notices the results!

The importance of a varied, accurate, current, exciting collection cannot be overstated. The collection and how it is handled keeps patrons coming back to the library. Without an outstanding collection, the library is just a building with dusty books. If the collection does not meet the needs of the patrons and entice them into learning, the building will soon feel antiquated and unnecessary. The collection should create a vibrant stimulating environment where students enjoy learning during their classes and on their own. The collection is the draw that attracts students and teachers alike so that real learning takes place with real resources that meet the needs of all the patrons.

In the current educational climate where test scores are so important, the school library must be in the forefront of providing the resources and instruction needed for students to succeed. More than 19 studies in states such as Colorado, North Carolina, and Florida have shown that there is a strong connection between schools with effective school libraries and higher student achievement. In other research

Collection development in today's library includes selecting digital resources such as online databases for electronic research.

Even a visually exciting library like this one will not live up to expectations without a dynamic collection that matches the room's appeal.

that asked students what they think of libraries, students have stated that the school library helps them complete homework assignments, helps them get better grades, and helps them by providing computers to improve their academic work. It is very evident that using the library collection to support reading programs as well as the entire school curriculum leads to better readers and higher test scores.

KNOW THE COLLECTION

The first step in selecting materials for your collection is to know what is already in the collection. Knowing the collection leads to understanding the collection's needs. Input is needed from all library staff as to what students and teachers need. It is important to purchase diverse materials in all academic subjects as well as in all areas of interest to the students. But with budgets tight and state standards changing, it is imperative to find out what is already in the collection so money is not wasted by purchasing similar or duplicate materials. One way to do that is to peruse the shelves. When shelving books, look to either side of the book that is being shelved to note if there are multiple books on a popular subject. Do resources show all viewpoints on a topic? Look at the books to see if they are worn. A book that shows a great deal of wear and tear may be a popular subject with students and may need to be replaced, or it could simply be an old book that simply needs to be discarded. Becoming more familiar with your collection and school community will help determine if a worn book merits replacement or should be removed from the collection. Which Dewey decimal numbers have no books or very few books? Maybe these are areas to focus on developing.

COLLECTION MAPPING

Analyzing the collection by observation is important, but it is also important to employ technology

FAQ
IS THERE ANY EVIDENCE THAT LIBRARIES AND THEIR COLLECTIONS MAKE A DIFFERENCE IN ACADEMIC ACHIEVEMENT?

Numerous state studies have shown that effective libraries have a strong positive impact on student test scores. Investigate these studies to learn more:

Frequently Asked Questions

Baumbach, Donna. *Making the Grade: The Status of School Library Media Centers in the Sunshine State and How They contribute to Student Achievement.* Salt Lake City, Utah: Hi Willow Research and Publishing, 2003. ISBN 093151097X.

Lance, Keith Curry, and David V. Loertscher. *Powering Achievement: School Library Media Programs Make a Difference: The Evidence.* Salt Lake City, Utah: Hi Willow Research and Publishing, 2001. ISBN: 0931510775.

Lance, Keith Curry, Marcia J. Rodney, and Christine Hamilton-Pennell. *How School Librarians Help Kids Achieve Standards: The Second Colorado Study.* Salt Lake City, Utah: Hi Willow Research and Publishers, 2000. ISBN: 0931510767.

How School Librarians Improve Outcomes for Children—The New Mexico Study. Salt Lake City, Utah: Hi Willow Research and Publishing, 2003. ISBN: 0931510872.

Rodney, Marcia J., Keith Curry Lance, and Christine Hamilton-Pennell. "The Impact of Michigan School Librarians on Academic Achievement: Kids Who Have Libraries Succeed." Michigan.gov. The Library of Michigan. 2003. http://www.michigan.gov/documents/hal_lm_schllibstudy03_76626_7.pdf (accessed January 21, 2011).

FAQ
DO I HAVE TO USE THE DEWEY DECIMAL SYSTEM?

Placing books on the shelves in Dewey decimal order has been a standard for many years. Throughout the years, many school libraries have considered different ways to shelve books. For example, some libraries consider arranging books by grade level or by the points designated by popular reading programs. But this does not teach children organizational skills. It also lends itself to "pigeon holing" children by not allowing them the opportunity to search for and read books below their level

Frequently Asked Questions

(which helps them learn to read faster) or above their level (which challenges their vocabulary and reading skills). Another idea is to arrange books by genres, such as mystery or romance. This may seem like a good idea; after all that is what they do in bookstores; however, schools are in the business of teaching as well as enticing children to read good books. By learning a standard system, the Dewey decimal system, students have a better understanding of organization and can find a book in any school, public, or college library.

FAQ
DO I HAVE TO BUY BOOKS FOR EVERY DEWEY DECIMAL NUMBER?

Frequently Asked Questions

Each number in the Dewey decimal system stands for a different subject area. Many times your school curriculum will not involve certain subjects. These numbers will naturally have few or no books in them. There is no reason to buy books that that no one will read so don't feel obligated to have books on every subject. Some numbers in the Dewey decimal system will not be used in all libraries.

FAQ
WHAT ARE THE DEWEY DECIMAL NUMBER CATEGORIES?

Frequently Asked Questions

Generalities	000
Philosophy and Psychology	100
Religion	200
Social Sciences	300
Language	400
Natural Sciences and Math	500
Technology (Applied Sciences)	600
The Arts	700
Literature	800
History and Geography	900

to get a clear visual picture of what is available to students. Most media management systems will create a report that will tell the age of your books as well as give current and past circulation statistics. After running a report, it is easy to see which Dewey decimal numbers have no materials. That is not necessarily a bad thing if the school curriculum is not involved in that area of study. Noting which materials have never been used, the decision can be made to promote these unused

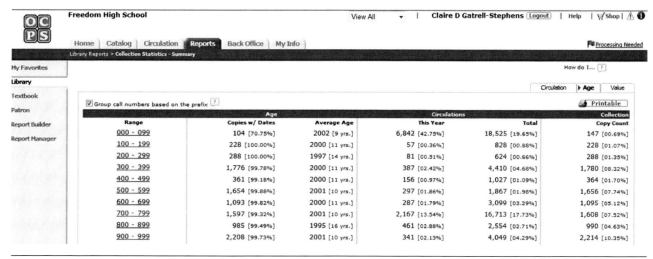

	Age		Circulations		Collection
Range	Copies w/ Dates	Average Age	This Year	Total	Copy Count
000 - 099	104 [70.75%]	2002 [9 yrs.]	6,842 [42.75%]	18,525 [19.65%]	147 [00.69%]
100 - 199	228 [100.00%]	2000 [11 yrs.]	57 [00.36%]	828 [00.88%]	228 [01.07%]
200 - 299	288 [100.00%]	1997 [14 yrs.]	81 [00.51%]	624 [00.66%]	288 [01.35%]
300 - 399	1,776 [99.78%]	2000 [11 yrs.]	387 [02.42%]	4,410 [04.68%]	1,780 [08.32%]
400 - 499	361 [99.18%]	2000 [11 yrs.]	156 [00.97%]	1,027 [01.09%]	364 [01.70%]
500 - 599	1,654 [99.88%]	2001 [10 yrs.]	297 [01.86%]	1,867 [01.98%]	1,656 [07.74%]
600 - 699	1,093 [99.82%]	2000 [11 yrs.]	287 [01.79%]	3,099 [03.29%]	1,095 [05.12%]
700 - 799	1,597 [99.32%]	2001 [10 yrs.]	2,167 [13.54%]	16,713 [17.73%]	1,608 [07.52%]
800 - 899	985 [99.49%]	1995 [16 yrs.]	461 [02.88%]	2,554 [02.71%]	990 [04.63%]
900 - 999	2,208 [99.73%]	2001 [10 yrs.]	341 [02.13%]	4,049 [04.29%]	2,214 [10.35%]

Reports such as this one generated by Follett's Destiny library management system help in understanding many things about the collection including its age, how many books are available in each area, and how often the books circulate.

FAQ
HOW DO I FIND OUT WHAT THE CURRICULUM IS AT EACH GRADE LEVEL IN MY SCHOOL?

First check your state Department of Education (DOE) website. Curriculum standards are given for each grade level. Then check your district website. Usually you will find benchmarks, which help you understand what students need to know by the end of each grade. Then talk to department chairs or teachers at your school. They will tell you what resources they use or need to make sure the students reach these benchmarks. For instance, students might need to "understand weather." Teachers may need nonfiction books and DVDs on the atmosphere, clouds, tornadoes, hurricanes, and so forth. They might want to read weather-related fiction books such as *Night of the Twisters* by Ivy Ruckman (an older book, but one of the best to describe the aftermath of a tornado). They may want to know about websites that have weather-related games in which students can learn about weather while playing a game. These are all important materials that you can provide to help teachers meet the curriculum standards for their grade levels.

Frequently Asked Questions

materials more or to discard them if they are not needed because of the school curriculum.

Another way to map your collection is to export library data to a vendor website where it will be analyzed and sent back in the form of graphs and charts. This is part of collection mapping and is easy and

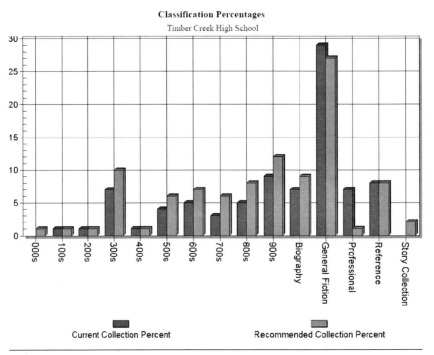

This graph provided by Mackin Educational Services comes from their collection mapping program. It shows the current holdings in a library collection by Dewey decimal number and compares the collection to the recommended numbers for each area.

completely free of cost. Exporting library files does not affect the data in any way and the analysis takes a matter of minutes. Contact favorite vendors or visit their websites for simple instructions on how to analyze your collection. There is an added bonus when using a website of a vendor that is commonly used for purchasing books for the school library. When making a list of books to buy on the website, the site will have a record of what has been previously ordered and the site will flag books and other products that have been ordered in the past. Precious budget funds may be wasted by buying the same books, or, on the other hand, multiple copies of that book might be needed because students love it. Consult the district librarian concerning these options.

Once this information has been gathered, start by noting what areas lack resources. Decide if those are the areas needing consideration when spending what little funds are available to the library. Collection mapping data can be used to show the principal, Parent Teacher Association (PTA), School Advisory Committee (SAC), or other groups who might have funds available for library use. But the best part of really knowing the collection is when that shy, quiet little student asks for a book that he wants to read and he is able to find it with the help of library staff!

FAQ
WHAT IS COLLECTION MAPPING?

Frequently Asked Questions

Collection mapping is a process of analyzing collections that looks at all the materials that are in a school library. Collection mapping looks at the number of materials in each Dewey area. Age of materials is also considered. In the past, this process was time-consuming; however, the advent of computer library management systems has made it easy. Most management software programs sort the collection data in a variety of ways that can easily show books and other materials in surprising detail. The program can explain your data, such as how many materials are available in each Dewey number. It can also show the age of the collection and how many times items have been checked out. Many vendors offer similar services that will download collection data and provide detailed statistics. Collection data can be manipulated to focus on small details; for example, a teacher may want to know how many books you have on chemical elements because she is thinking of assigning a chemistry project and wants to know what books would be available for students to use. By focusing media management software tools specifically on the Dewey number 546, it is possible to quickly get a snapshot of available materials on the subject.

These software programs also produce colorful and easy-to-read charts that help the library staff and others visualize the state of the collection. Programs compare the school's collection with other schools in the district. This is useful information to share with the principal, PTA, School Advisory Council (SAC), or district level staff. Enlist teachers to help present this information. Administrators and school groups often have funding available but must validate expenditures. The collection mapping data will help them justify providing money for new materials at the school.

KNOW YOUR STUDENTS

Before developing your collection, it is necessary to really know your students. Each school in each district may teach the same subjects, but the students are vastly different. School statistics will show student reading levels, racial and ethnic information, and socioeconomic data, but statistics only tell part of the picture. Engage with your school's children to learn about their lives, their interests, and their hopes for the future. Find out which students are special needs students by asking questions of the students' teacher or the exceptional education teachers. By talking to students as a class or one-on-one, it is easy to learn how much they know about the subjects taught at their grade level, which will in turn influence which and how many materials need to be purchased to support those subjects. Hold an impromptu reference interview with students to learn more about their needs.

FAQ
HOW MANY COPIES OF THE SAME TITLE SHOULD THERE BE ON THE SHELVES?

Frequently Asked Questions

For nonfiction books, one copy of each title is sufficient. If many materials are needed on the same subject because classes often study that topic area, buy different titles so that students are able to get many different perspectives. Buying too many books that are exactly the same will date the collection. Every year new books are published on popular topics so it is important to update subject areas frequently.

Sometimes it is advisable to buy multiple copies of popular fiction books. The rule of thumb is to buy no more than five copies of a particular book. It is wise to purchase both hardbacks and paperbacks. Generally the paperback copies will not last as long, so by the time the demand for that popular title begins to fall, the paperback copies will probably need to be discarded, leaving one or two copies for the shelf. If it is necessary to buy more copies because an upcoming contest will require lots of books, create a plan for when the contest is over. Could a drawing be held for the extra books? Could the extras be given to teachers for their classroom libraries? There are lots of creative ways to make use of surplus copies, and the teachers and students will be glad to take surplus library items.

Becoming familiar with the collection helps library staff provide students with the books they love.

Schools today have diverse student populations at all levels. It is important that the library collection represent all members of the school community.

FAQ
WHAT IS A REFERENCE INTERVIEW?

When a student comes to the library and asks for help, the collection of questions asked by the library staff is known as a *reference interview.* Many times students ask for what they think that they want, but not what they really need to complete their project. By asking a few quick questions, it is easy to determine the information needed to help the student. Remember to use the best customer service attitude possible during the reference interview. Students who feel comfortable will answer questions completely and truthfully, making it easy to understand what the student needs.

Frequently Asked Questions

Learning students' interests will help determine what fiction and nonfiction books to buy. For instance, if many students love horses, there are many series that will appeal to them. By the same token, urban school students might be interested in entirely different topics.

Talking to children directly helps you find out what they want everyone to know, but intently observing students will reveal even more about them. Talking to students about what subjects they like to read about and at what level they are most comfortable reading will result in finding out students' true reading patterns. Listening to students

Table **1.1** Use School Demographics to Learn About Your Students

Racial/ethnic group	Number of students enrolled in October		School %		District %		State %	
	Female	Male	2009–2010	2008–2009	2009–2010	2008–2009	2009–2010	2008–2009
White	27	21	8.2	9.8	32.8	33.6	44.4	45.3
Black	28	25	9.1	10.0	27.3	27.3	23.0	23.0
Hispanic	223	240	79.6	76.5	32.2	31.3	26.2	25.0
Asian	4	4	0.7	0.3	4.5	4.3	2.6	2.5
American Indian		1	0.2	0.2	0.4	0.4	0.3	0.3
Multiracial	8	5	2.2	3.3	2.8	3.0	3.4	3.9
Disabled	23	54	13.2	14.6	12.9	13.4	14.1	14.3
Economically disadvantaged	256	251	87.1	81.6	50.9	48.6	53.5	49.6
English Language Learners (ELL)	155	175	56.7	58.4	22.8	23.3	11.6	11.8
Migrant					0.1	0.2	0.5	0.5
Female	286		49.1	46.9	48.7	48.8	48.7	48.7
Male		296	50.9	53.1	51.3	51.2	51.3	51.3
Total	582		100.0	100.0	100.0	100.0	100.0	100.0

This table from the Florida State Department of Education shows the ethnic and socioeconomic make up of an elementary school. By studying this information you will learn many things. For instance, the majority of the students at this school are Hispanic, and there is a high percentage of English language learners. This information will help guide purchasing for the school library; for example, you may want to purchase bilingual books in both Spanish and English to help English language learners. This type of data is commonly available from your state department of education or district office. Ask your administrator if you would like assistance understanding the demographic make-up of your school.

TOP TEN QUESTIONS TO ASK IN A REFERENCE INTERVIEW

Top 10 reasons why you should...

1. Why do you need this information? (A project for school? Personal information?)
2. What sources have you already tried to get the information that you need?
3. How much information do you need? How long or in-depth does your project need to be?
4. Do you have an assignment sheet and rubric? When is the project due?
5. Have you checked the online card catalog?
6. Do you need to read an entire book or can you use articles from magazines or newspapers?
7. Would you rather use web-based resources?
8. Do you have resources at home (e.g., books or computer access?)?
9. Do you like to read or is reading not your favorite thing to do? (This question helps ascertain reading level.)
10. (A question for after you've helped the student.) Did you find the information that you were looking for?

talking to their peers will give insights as to books they have read, movies they have seen, or their leisure interests. Fiction books especially are written to so many audiences. Learn about the students to determine which they will like. Learning about patrons makes the job of deciding what should be part of your collection easier. There is no reason to buy a book that is a bestseller but no student would ever read. Just because a book is an award winner does not mean it is right for the students in your school community.

Another way to find out what the students would like to have in their library is to ask them! Prepare a very short survey and ask teachers to have their students fill it out. Students like to fill out questionnaires for a small treat. The information gained will be more than worth the effort. Ask questions about what they like to do, their favorite sport, and the best book they have ever read. These results will determine decisions about future purchases. (The sample student survey provided here is designed for high school students.)

KNOW YOUR CURRICULUM

School libraries exist to support student learning, so being educated about the curriculum will support collection development efforts.

FAQ
HOW DO I FIND MATERIALS ON DIFFERENT SUBJECTS THAT INTEREST MY STUDENTS?

Frequently Asked Questions

Search the district media management program to find out what materials other schools in the district have on the topic needed. Check vendor websites. Many websites allow searches by topic and level. Peruse bookstore shelves to find out if there are any new books on the topic needed. Check out what is new at the local public library. They have personnel whose job is to buy the best new books for children.

Another tip! Refer to professional journals for school librarians such as *Library Media Connection, School Library Monthly*, or *Booklist.* Most journals have reviews or feature lesson plans and activities that contain suggested resources to support the lessons. There are many excellent professional journals available from a variety of groups such as the American Library Association or your local state professional group. Ask several school librarians in the area for their preferred review sources and then examine their suggestions to find ones that would appeal to teachers at the school.

There are also websites that can help locate titles as well. For example, http://hbook.com/Default.asp, the website for *Horn Book* magazine, contains links to the *Horn Book* guide that has an online searchable database of over 80,000 titles. For older students try *TeenReads.com* (http://www.teenreads.com), a website sponsored by *Book Report* magazine that focuses on young adult trends. Try doing a simple web search on "children's book reviews," but be careful; many of the websites that appear with this type of search will be companies that want to sell their books, something reputable review sites do not do.

FAQ
HOW ARE AWARD-WINNING BOOKS CHOSEN?

Frequently Asked Questions

Each award has its own criteria. For instance, the Newbery Award is given each year to the best children's book of the year. But the website reveals that the book has to have been published during the preceding year. The website also explains that the book must be written in English by a citizen or resident of the United States. Check www.ala.org for more criteria for this and other prestigious awards.

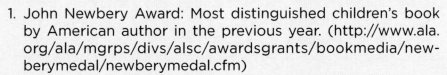

TOP TEN AWARDS FOR BOOKS

In truth, there is no real "top ten" list of book awards. This list represents some of the most popular awards that have benefitted the authors of this book in their collection development work.

Top 10 reasons why you should...

1. John Newbery Award: Most distinguished children's book by American author in the previous year. (http://www.ala. org/ala/mgrps/divs/alsc/awardsgrants/bookmedia/new- berymedal/newberymedal.cfm)
2. Caldecott Medal: Most distinguished picture book by American author in the previous year. (http://www.ala.org/ala/mgrps/divs/alsc/awardsgrants/bookme- dia/caldecottmedal/caldecottmedal.cfm)
3. Michael L. Printz Award: Best young adult book of the year. (http://www.ala.org/ ala/mgrps/divs/yalsa/booklistsawards/printzaward/Printz.cfm)
4. Alex Award: Top ten adult books that have appeal for young adults. (http://www. ala.org/ala/mgrps/divs/yalsa/booklistsawards/alexawards/alexawards.cfm)
5. William A Morris YA Award: Best book published by a first-time author for teens. (http://www.ala.org/ala/mgrps/divs/yalsa/booklistsawards/morris/morri saward.cfm)
6. Coretta Scott King Book Award: This award is given to African American authors and illustrators in recognition of work that promotes understanding and appre- ciation of the culture of all peoples and their contribution to the realization of the American dream for all people. (http://www.ala.org/ala/mgrps/rts/emiert/ cskbookawards/recipients.cfm)
7. Pura Belpre Medal: Book that most celebrates Latino culture by a Latino author. (http://www.ala.org/ala/mgrps/divs/alsc/awardsgrants/bookmedia/bel premedal/index.cfm)
8. Siebert Medal: Most distinguished information book published in English in the previous year. (http://www.ala.org/ala/mgrps/divs/alsc/awardsgrants/bookme dia/sibertmedal/index.cfm)
9. Geisel Award: Most distinguished American book for beginning readers in the previous year. (http://www.ala.org/ala/mgrps/divs/alsc/awardsgrants/bookme dia/geiselaward/index.cfm)
10. Scott O'Dell Award: Best historical fiction published in the previous year for children or young adults. (http://www.scottodell.com/pages/ScottO'DellAwardf orHistoricalFiction.aspx)

Talking with teachers promotes good feelings toward the library pro- gram and also gives information about how the teachers teach their classes. Asking them what they need to teach the subjects they must teach will inform the staff about the resources patrons need. Talking to teachers is a way to find out what new books, audiovisual, and on- line resources are available to support their plans. Giving teachers

FAQ
WHAT IF STUDENTS REQUEST GRAPHIC NOVELS? AREN'T THEY JUST COMIC BOOKS?

Frequently Asked Questions

Much has been written about graphic novels, and it is generally believed that the graphic novel is a valuable book format that helps reluctant readers develop fluency and comprehension when reading. The belief is that if students consistently read graphic novels, they will soon turn to higher level texts, increasing their reading levels. Please note this warning: The content of graphic novels can sometimes be violent and sexual. Many times students will ask for titles that may not be appropriate for the school level. Become friends with the local bookstore workers. Many of them read graphic novels and can help with decisions on which books to buy. Or ask a reliable student to help. This will make the student feel special and will help with purchasing decisions at the same time.

input and showing them materials that are available will encourage teachers to use the library and the resources in the collection.

Learning exactly what makes up the curriculum is easy. Read the state standards or school district curriculum (usually found on your district or state website) in order to understand what concepts must be covered in each grade. Do fifth grade social studies students study ancient Egypt or your state history? Do third grade science students study bugs or inventions? Reading the table of contents of textbooks will also help clarify what information teachers are using to teach the skills necessary for their students to be successful. Teachers need resources to support that teaching. Students will be creating projects while they are studying mandated topics. The collection should support subjects taught and hopefully excite students so much that they want to read more information about the topics the teachers are introducing.

When formulating a survey for the students, create one for the teachers too. Teachers appreciate the ability to give input on library purchases. Ask them what they like about the collection and what topics need to be covered in more depth. Ask them what part of the collection helps their instruction and what materials they need to take instruction to the next level. Many times when a survey is created, questions are posed that inform the survey participant of information they don't know. Don't forget to put reminders in the survey about resources teachers may have forgotten are available for them. These surveys promote communication with your teachers, and because they are anonymous, you can find out how teachers really feel about your library resources. All of this data will help in justifying your purchases

LIBRARY STUDENT SURVEY

It is the goal of the library staff to offer all the resources and services that will help you be successful in your studies and enrich your reading enjoyment. Please help us by completing this survey. Circle the one answer that best answers the questions below. Feel free to make additional comments in the margins or on the back of this survey. Your input is important to us!

Grade level: Freshmen   Sophomore   Junior   Senior

How often do you visit the library *per week* outside of class time?

Never   1 to 3 times   4 to 7 times   7 to 10 times   Almost every day

When do you most often visit the library outside of class time?

Before school   During lunch   After school   I don't

What are the most common purposes for your visits to the library? (circle all that apply)

Work on class assignments, Research, Read, Copy machine, Die cut machine, Play cards, Check out books for class, Use computers for class work or research, Check out books for pleasure reading, Use the computers for games and unrelated school work, Just to hang out with friends, I only visit when a teacher brings the class, Other
_____

How often do you visit the county public library *per month*?

Never   1 to 3 times   4 to 7 times   7 to 10 times   On a weekly basis

Please list two or three of your favorite fiction authors or titles:

_____

_____

What do you prefer to check out most:

Paperback books   Hardcover books   Doesn't matter

Please list two or three of your favorite fiction authors or titles:

_____

_____

Think about the research you did this year. From your experience in the library, what types of nonfiction topics do we need to help you with research for your classes?

Examples: Books on drugs, prehistoric life, political leaders, etc.

What Internet resources did you use in your research? Circle all that apply.

Google, Ask.com, Yahoo, Wikipedia, Infotrac by Gale (Literature, Biography, Student Resource Center, or Opposing Viewpoints), World Book Online, Grolier Online, Nettrekker, Britannica Online, CountryWatch, Other _____

Write any additional comments or suggestions on the back of this paper. Thanks for your help!

Table 1.2 Using State Standards in Collection Development

Sample fifth grade social studies standards	How a media specialist might use the standards in collection development
Use primary and secondary sources to understand history.	Be sure to purchase books and online data bases that include primary source materials for all areas of the social studies curriculum.
Compare cultural aspects of ancient American civilizations (Aztecs/Mayas; Mound Builders/Anasazi/Inuit).	Ancient native civilizations of the Americas are clearly identified in this standard. Be sure to purchase books, DVDs, etc., that focus on each group. Check with teachers to identify other groups not mentioned in the standard.
Compare characteristics of New England, Middle, and Southern colonies.	This standard refers to the original 13 American colonies during the prerevolutionary period. State books and related media may have some information, but nonfiction books related to Colonial America and the individual colonies during that era would be best.

Source: Next Generation Sunshine State Standards, Florida Department of Education, available at http://www.floridastandards.org/Standards/FLStandardSearch.aspx.

FAQ
HOW CAN A SURVEY GIVE THE SURVEY TAKERS INFORMATION?

Frequently Asked Questions

Depending on what questions are created, surveys can enlighten survey takers. For instance, if teachers are asked how many times they have used your professional materials, you might find that some teachers didn't even know that professional materials were available in the library. These materials may have been purchased by the learning specialist, curriculum resource teacher, or administrators. If students are asked how many audiobooks they have checked out in the past year, they may be alerted for the first time to the fact that audiobooks are available for checkout.

HIGH SCHOOL FACULTY SURVEY

Please help us to help you. Fill out this short survey to let us know how we are doing and how we can serve you better. Please return this completed form to your media specialists.

1. Do you use the media center for . . .? (Check all that apply)

    ___ Entire class checking out books
    ___ Individual passes
    ___ Research using books
    ___ Research using computers
    ___ Meetings
    ___ I have never sent students or brought students to the media center.

2. A media specialist has assisted my class by . . .? (Check all that apply)

    ___ Collaborating and helping teach a research unit.
    ___ Giving book talks to encourage reading.
    ___ Helping facilitate a contest to encourage literacy skills.
    ___ Locating materials and sending them to my classroom.
    ___ Conducting professional training.
    ___ Other _____

3. My students use the online databases offered by the Media Center.

    ___Often   ___Sometimes   ___Never

4. Do you have the technology you need in the classroom to facilitate learning?

    ___ Yes, I have all I need.
    ___ No, I need the following items for my classroom _____

5. When I check out AV equipment from the media center . . .

    ___ It is always available and works well.
    ___ We need more equipment because what I want is always checked out.
    ___ What I want is not available. It is _____.
    ___ I never check out equipment from the media center.

6. Does our print collection (books, magazines, newspapers) meet your needs?

    ___ Yes, I find lots of materials on all topics.
    ___ No, we need more information on _____.
    ___ I never read books or assign them to my students.

7. I take advantage of these media services. (Check all that apply)

    ___ Laminating   ___ Bulletin Board Paper
    ___ Material Requests (books, magazines, and videos)

__ Die cuts (shapes/letters)	__ Scantron/Edusoft
__ Locate materials using Destiny	__ Reserving materials for classes

8. Does our non-print collection (DVDs, audiobooks) meet your needs?

    __ Yes, I find lots of materials on all topics.

    __ No, we need more information on _____.

    __ I never watch videos in my class.

    __ I never use audiobooks.

9. I peruse the Media Center's professional materials . . .

    ___Often   ___Sometimes   __I don't even know where it is!

10. Do you use the class sets of novels available in the media center?

    ___Often   ___Sometimes   __Never

Please comment on our . . .

Strengths _____

Weaknesses _____

and budget requests to the school administrator and district library personnel.

KNOW YOUR SCHOOL COMMUNITY

When looking for volunteers for the many jobs that need to be done in the media center, remember the students' parents. Sometimes parents are just waiting to be asked to lend a hand. The school's PTA may have available funds that can be requested. Parents like to see their

Parent volunteers can be a great resource in your library.

FAQ
HOW DO PARENTS AND COMMUNITY MEMBERS GET INVOLVED IN THE LIBRARY PROGRAM?

Talk to parent groups such as the PTA. Sometimes parents are just volunteers waiting to be asked. Many times nearby businesses are looking for ways to get their employees involved in community service. Talk to managers of nearby businesses to find out if they are interested in helping your school. Target stores are noted for their volunteering. When someone at a school writes a Target grant, one grant question even asks how their volunteers would be able to help with the implementation of the grant.

Frequently Asked Questions

TOP TEN WAYS TO INVOLVE PARENTS

Top 10 reasons why you should...

1. Ask them to host a book fair.
2. Ask them to host a literacy night.
3. Ask them to donate a book for their child's birthday. Make sure you put a nameplate on the inside cover that says something like "This book donated in honor of John Smith's 10th birthday."
4. Ask them to donate a book for their child's graduation from elementary school or middle school or high school.
5. Ask them to donate time each week to help you with library organization or other clerical tasks.
6. Ask them to be guest readers once a week for different classes.
7. Ask them to be guest speakers on their professions or their hobbies.
8. Ask them to arrange a book fair for your library at a local bookstore.
9. Ask them to help you organize a book preview of all the books you have purchased during the year. This could be a small breakfast, a luncheon, or snacks during a faculty meeting with all your new materials displayed for teachers to see.
10. Ask them to solicit nearby businesses for coupons that you can give students as incentives for reading.

hard-earned money going to a cause that benefits the entire school. Many parents are also willing to volunteer their time to help. Some parents want to be on a schedule; for example, they might prefer to help every Tuesday morning. Some would rather have activities that they can organize and that culminate in a short time, such as book fairs or reading nights. These parents are invaluable when putting on a highly successful activity. Connecting these parents to teachers and administrators at the school will benefit the library in the long run.

At many schools, most parents work or do not have the inclination to volunteer. Don't be afraid to ask community members for help. High school students are often looking for volunteer hours and love to work with children or help organize the library. Retired teachers often miss children and are looking for ways to help the community. Don't overlook their expertise with children and with the curriculum. Senior citizens are also often looking for volunteer opportunities. "Grandma's Story Time" could turn into a weekly activity that kindergartener's would certainly enjoy!

CHAPTER 2
DEVELOPING A COLLECTION PLAN

Creating a collection development plan using the information gathered from surveys and collection analysis may be time-consuming, but it is necessary. If the school doesn't already have a collection development policy, check with district librarians to determine if there is an overall district policy in place. That policy can easily be adapted to each unique school. If the district does not have a written plan, look online and find a plan from another school system. Print it out and use this as a starting place. Make small or large adjustments, depending on the needs of your school. It is important to have something in writing so that when money becomes available, the rationale for using the money wisely is in place.

FAQ
HOW CAN I LOCATE SAMPLE COLLECTION DEVELOPMENT POLICIES ON THE WEB?

Frequently Asked Questions

A simple web search using your favorite search engine will bring up many samples. Try using "school library collection development policy" as your search term. Including the quotation marks around the phrase will tell the search engine you are looking for that specific phrase.

Here are a few collection development policy websites:

INDIVIDUAL SCHOOLS

The Jewish Day School, Bellevue, Washington: http://www.jds.org/welcome-to-the-library/collection-development-policy

Apponequet Regional High School Library, Lakeville, Massachusetts: http://users.rcn.com/libra/mission.html

Slauson Middle School, Ann Arbor, Michigan: http://slauson.a2schools.org/slauson.home/media_center

Westwood Elementary, Fairview, Tennessee: http://www.wcs.edu/wes/Media/collection.htm

SCHOOL DISTRICTS

Hopkinton School District, Contoocook, New Hampshire: http://www.hopkinton
    schools.org/hhs/library/selpol.html

Orange County Public Schools, Orlando, Florida: http://mediacenter.ocps.net/hand
    book/colldev.htm

School District of Philadelphia, Philadelphia, Pennsylvania: http://www.hopkinton
    schools.org/hhs/library/selpol.html

Remember, your policy does not have to be exactly like these. Your collection development policy can be as simple or complex as is required to be to reflect the needs of your school and community.

Make sure that there are stated goals in the library when developing a collection plan. Of course, it is necessary to create short-term goals, such as putting up the display for George Washington's birthday or processing all the free books just received from the book fair. But long-range goals are necessary too. When talking to the principal about these long-range goals, he knows that working in the library is more

TOP TEN SAMPLE SHORT-TERM GOALS FOR OCTOBER

Top 10 reasons why you should...

Creating monthly goals helps you stay focused while working in your school library. This is a list of possible goals for the month of October.

1. Survey fifth grade to find out what kind of fiction books they want me to buy.
2. Put up a display for Columbus Day and a display for scary books (Halloween).
3. Take down Hispanic Month (September 15 to October 15) display.
4. Begin book order.
5. Have first meeting of the Library Club (students who help in the library).
6. Touch base with teachers who might want to schedule their classes for time to use library resources.
7. Take inventory of supplies in case an order is needed.
8. Weed one section of the shelves.
9. Evaluate check-out procedures. (Can check-out be more efficient? Does the desk need to be changed in any way?)
10. Create monthly bulletin board display. (Maybe Guess Who? With pictures of teachers in Halloween costumes when they were children.)

than just a job. He will see the concern to make the library as effective as possible for the children. It is always a good idea to jot down a list of items needing to be accomplished each week or month. Working in a school library often becomes hectic and there are frequent interruptions. A list often helps to keep staff focused.

FAQ
HOW WILL MY PRINCIPAL KNOW WHAT MY GOALS ARE?

Meet with your principal periodically, but remember that she is probably not interested in your short-term goals. These will be evident when she looks around the media center or sees the programs that are happening in the media center. A short e-mail at the beginning of the year outlining your long-term goals will let her know that you plan to promote the school library as a learning environment. Copying her on e-mails will allow her to see that you are still working on those goals.

Frequently Asked Questions

BEGIN WITH THE END IN MIND

As the school year begins, think of what the end of the year will look like. Will the shelves have more books about the lives of famous historical and contemporary figures for that teacher who always assigns the children a biography project in fourth grade? Will third grade students spend more time using databases provided to the school by your district? Will this year see a rise in participation in reading the state's list of award-winning books? Not all states select a list of reading books each year, but it is possible to borrow a list from another state. Create displays, competitions, and prizes for children who read these books. If it is unclear which goals would benefit students most, engage teachers in conversation. Asking their help gives them "buy in." When a teacher mentions that she is going to read Flat Stanley books to her class and ask them to send a "Stanley" to their friends and relatives all over the country, it will be necessary to provide her with a lot of books on states and countries. This project may lead the staff to look at that area of the collection and decide that the long-term goal for that year is to "beef up" the 900s section of the library. Maybe the books about states are outdated and maybe books are not even available on every country Stanley might visit. Take a hard look at that area of the collection and spend the year looking for books that would make that area of the collection more current and appealing to the students. There are many outstanding databases that have excellent information on

Online subscriptions such as netTrekker (http://www.nettrekker.com) are frequently purchased by schools and districts to help students locate safe, relevant digital resources and information.

FAQ
HOW DO I FIND OUT ABOUT READING LISTS FROM OTHER STATES?

Frequently Asked Questions

The Internet is a great place to look for current state reading lists. Just query the state you are interested in and ask for their book lists. You will find state reading lists and other materials on how to use the books. You will begin to notice some books are on multiple lists. That should tell you that those are books you want to look at to purchase for your students.

states and countries. Consider purchasing one of these. If funds are short, investigate free websites that contain the information needed. Make sure the site is authoritative, accurate, up-to-date, and accessible to students. Encourage students to learn about other countries by checking books out and learning more about the databases available for research.

FLORIDA TEEN READS NOMINEES 2012-2013

Bedford, Martyn. *Flip*.

Condie, Ally. *Matched*.

de la Pena, Matt. *I Will Save You*.

Flinn, Alex. *Cloaked*.

Grennan, Conor. *Little Princes: One Man's Promise to Bring Home the Lost Children of Nepal*.

Hautman, Pete. *Blank Confession*.

Herbach, Geoff. *Stupid Fast*.

Johnson, Maureen. *The Name of the Star*.

King, A. S. *Please Ignore Vera Dietz*.

Maberry, Jonathon. *Rot & Ruin*.

Matson, Morgan. *Amy & Roger's Epic Detour*.

Nelson, Blake. *Recovery Road*.

Resau, Laura. *The Queen of Water*.

Revis, Beth. *Across the Universe*.

Roth, Veronica. *Divergent*.

State reading lists such as the Florida State Teens Read list shown here are easy to find using a simple Internet search. Lists can also be located using links from publisher and vendor websites that market the list's titles.

From *School Library Collection Development: Just the Basics* by Claire Gatrell Stephens and Patricia Franklin. Santa Barbara, CA: Libraries Unlimited. Copyright © 2012.

FAQ
IF I BEGIN A CONTEST USING A STATE LIST OF BOOKS (MINE OR ANOTHER STATE), HOW MANY BOOKS OF EACH TITLE SHOULD I BUY?

Frequently Asked Questions

The number of books of each title that are purchased depends on the size of the school and the amount of funds available. Five to ten books of each paperback is advisable. If the books are only published as hardbacks, use your best judgment. Many schools buy at least one hardback that will last a long time, and several paperbacks so that they can be used during the year the book is popular because it is on the state list. Buy as many as needed for the contest and as allowed by your budget.

Flat Stanley is a book by Jeff Brown. In the story Stanley makes himself flat and travels around the world via the mail. Many elementary teachers use the story to help children learn about other states and countries by having their students create their own Flat Stanley. Students mail their creation to friends and relatives. In this photo, a Flat Sally reads the local newspaper while visiting one of the authors in Florida.

FAQ
WHY DO I NEED TO MAKE LONG-TERM GOALS TOO? HOW ARE THEY DIFFERENT FROM THE SHORT-TERM GOALS I ALREADY MADE?

Short-term goals are those that can be accomplished in a brief period of time. These can be weekly or monthly goals. They make a big difference in day-to-day happenings in your school library. Short-term goals can make you more receptive to students and teachers and their needs, but long-term goals make an even bigger difference. Long-term goals are ideas that you want to implement, but that may take you the entire year to accomplish. These are changes that you want to make in order to make your library more effective in terms of real student achievement. Here are three sample long-term goals:

Frequently Asked Questions

1. To increase and update the country and state section of the library.
2. To evaluate the arrangement of tables and furniture in the school library to determine if the room is arranged effectively for teacher instruction.
3. To begin a library club of students who will stay after school, talk about books, and help with library tasks.

SELECTION POLICIES

Districts usually have written policies on how to select materials to purchase for your library. If these policies are unavailable, look at websites of larger or more proactive districts to get ideas. These policies include guidelines in such areas as where to find titles to buy. It is very

FAQ
WHAT IS THE DIFFERENCE BETWEEN A COLLECTION PLAN AND A SELECTION PLAN?

A collection plan includes procedures to identify needs, purchase items needed, and get those items to your users. A collection plan usually includes a selection plan. A selection plan is a policy that identifies criteria that you use to decide what to purchase. After you have identified weak areas in your collection, you use this policy to choose what items best meet these needs. With the large amount of items available to you, your selection policy helps to focus your buying and can serve as a rationale for your purchases in case anyone disagrees with them.

Frequently Asked Questions

important to select materials that are recommended by a reliable source such as *School Library Journal, Library Media Connection*, or *School Library Monthly* magazines. It is also possible to look at vendor's websites to search for a list of books on the subject. Be careful to note who has reviewed the books and what the reviewers wrote. This will give justification for whatever you order.

Going to a bookstore and buying books that look good is not a selection policy. But going to a bookstore and getting ideas is always fun. Many times the critical acclaim for the book is written on the cover so, while browsing, it is possible to find titles that are just right for students. At the same time, the source for the positive comments you find on the book jacket must be checked. Be sure it is from a reliable source and not the publisher's publicity department. When examining books in the bookstore, don't forget to notice things like the copyright date for currency or the layout and design of the book for readability; as the

Table 2.1 Sample Selection Policy Statement

Sample Selection Policy

Your selection policy statement might include several parts, such as selection criteria, selection standards for various media, or specific selection tools. Your policy needs to reflect the school community you serve and may include more or less information as required by your situation. Below is a sample of a brief selection policy.

Selection Criteria

In general, materials shall be selected based on their ability to enrich the curriculum of the school. Materials should provide a wide range of difficulty levels and appeal to different groups and ages in the school population. Differing points of view should be presented. Resources should be selected based on their strengths and literary and artistic merit. The following criteria are used as a guide in selection:

- The materials accurately represents current knowledge, ideas, and concepts of its subject matter. They are educationally significant.
- The material addresses current needs of the media center collection.
- The material is relevant to the curriculum.
- The material has received favorable reviews from standard sources or has been recommended by professionals with expertise in the area.
- The material contains quality writing or production values and is affordable.
- The resource comes from a reputable publisher, author, or vendor.
- The material is appealing and will be easily read and understood by students.
- The material contributes a diversity of ideas on subjects that may be controversial without resorting to "name-calling" or condemnation of opposing viewpoints.

---

old saying goes, you can't judge a book by its cover alone. It is also important to remember that bookstores generally do not stock a great deal of nonfiction for students. In order to preview nonfiction titles, in addition to a bookstore, pay a visit to the local public library and examine their books on the subject. Websites such as the American Library Association site (www.ala.org) are good places to look for titles of quality literature. Award-winning books are usually a good bet. Often vendors will try to entice customers to spend their money on vendor offerings. Some vendors can introduce books that are perfect for children and others will try to sell old titles that they are trying to eliminate. Don't allow a salesman to talk you into buying resources you do not want or need. Talk to your district librarians or other school librarians in the district. Use best judgment and the school will end up with great books that students will love.

TOP TEN WAYS TO IDENTIFY POSSIBLE RESOURCES FOR YOUR COLLECTION!

Even with an excellent selection policy, you may feel overwhelmed by the number of resources available for you to choose from. Here are some additional ideas to help you in your selection process.

Top 10 reasons why you should...

1. Read reviews in professional magazines like *School Library Journal* or *Library Media Connection.*
2. Check with your teachers and administration about curriculum changes and needs.
3. Read publisher websites to find out what new books are being published. Read blogs about books kids like to read.
4. Spend time in your local bookstore and public library. Examine books and other resources for ideas.
5. Ask students and teachers for suggestions. (You might put a suggestion box at your circulation desk and ask students to let you know if they want a particular title.)
6. Read books published for the age group at your school.
7. Ask parents to e-mail you titles that they would like their children to read.
8. Read newspaper reviews on children's books.
9. Talk to other schools and find out what books their students check out the most.
10. Determine which classic books need to be replaced.

Table 2.2 Sample Book Request Form

Book Request
If we do not have a book in our library that you think we should get, please fill in this form!
Title of the book you want
Author's name (if you know it)
Your name (optional)
Today's date
When we get the book, would you like us to check it out to you and deliver it to your classroom? (Circle your choice)
Yes   No

Note: A form like this allows students and teachers to submit titles for possible purchase.

The audiovisual collection should also be carefully selected with student learning goals in mind.

Audiovisual materials are often housed in the media center. These also need to be screened and selected with academics in mind. Many teachers know that students who are visual learners will retain information longer if the information is reinforced with a visual. As students more frequently use digital sources for information, they are more familiar with visual learning. A 10-minute clip from a nature video may show a science concept that the teacher has been trying to explain in several lessons. The ability to see the people and places of a historical era that the teacher is explaining will help put historical references in perspective and help struggling readers. Students may find it easier to understand a book if they listen to the audio as they read

FAQ
WHAT IF A TEACHER WANTS ME TO BUY A PARTICULAR DVD TO SHOW IN HER CLASSROOM?

Frequently Asked Questions

For copyright purposes, DVDs shown in the classroom should be purchased with performance rights. A teacher should not just show a DVD because it is Friday and the kids need a break. National copyright laws say a teacher may show a video if it applies to curriculum. However, unless you have purchased the performance rights, you have broken copyright by showing it in the classroom. There are companies who sell rights to show movies produced by many big production companies, such as *Movie USA*. You might look into these types of companies to avoid problems if your teachers want to show movies they have purchased on their own. It is also a good idea to investigate your school district's policies regarding the use of videos in the classroom. Many districts have strict use policies that must be followed by teachers and impact how schools purchase videos. Talk to district librarians and administrators at your school as to what your role should be in upholding copyright laws. Ultimately, our job is not to police teachers; that is an administrative task.

along. For these reasons, using audiovisual materials is now more important than ever.

Your collection will need to include equipment that teachers can use to play the DVDs or audio CDs. Ideally all teachers should have that equipment in their classroom, but if budgets do not permit that, equipment may have to be purchased, maintained, and inventoried by the library. There are usually district policies and contracts involved with the purchase of audiovisual equipment; be familiar with your district's policies. Many schools are now opting to show short videos from the Internet that fit their curriculum. Some schools purchase a video streaming option such as Discovery Education (http://www.dis coveryeducation.com/) or SAFARI Montage (http://safarimontage. com), which allows teachers to download videos to use in their classroom. This alleviates the need to purchase videos and give teachers a safe educational way to meet the needs of visual learners.

Selection considerations are many. Every school is unique and materials should be selected to match the school's curriculum and student needs.

Safari Montage is one of several video streaming services currently available to schools.

FAQ
HOW DO I SHELVE AUDIOVISUAL MATERIALS?

Audiobooks, DVDs, CDs, and so forth, are labeled and shelved in the same way books are shelved. In this way, teachers can find materials using the same numbers that they use when they are looking for print sources on particular subjects.

Frequently Asked Questions

FAQ
WHAT IS COPYRIGHT?

Copyright is the U.S. law that protects those who have created *intellectual property*. Original works such as books, movies, music, and other types of artwork are covered by the law. The 1976 Copyright Act protects authors from others who want to copy their work or make derivatives of them. Use the U.S. Copyright Office's website (http://www.copyright.gov/title17/) to read the entire law including its amendments since 1976. It is also a good idea to check up on your district's policies regarding the use of copyrighted works so that your purchases stay in compliance with district rules.

Frequently Asked Questions

TOP TEN SAMPLE SELECTION CONSIDERATIONS FOR AUDIOVISUAL RESOURCES

There are many things to consider when purchasing audiovisual materials for your library. Here are 10 important questions to consider during your selection process.

Top 10 reasons why you should...

1. Is the material of high quality?
2. Does it fit in with your curriculum?
3. Is it appropriate for your students based on age and community standards?
4. Is the audio or video in a format your equipment can support?
5. Is the material on the level your students can understand?
6. Does this material match your curriculum or the interests of your students?
7. Does the material support all viewpoints?
8. Is this the best price available and are you purchasing performance rights?
9. Is the material up to date?
10. Is the material accurate?

ETHICAL ISSUES

It is important to take into account the legal and moral obligation to students when you select materials. Students and parents rely on library staff to provide multiple resources on a subject that show all viewpoints. Even if personnel are adamantly against a particular viewpoint on a controversial subject, they are obligated to purchase resources that include all viewpoints. Remember to consider the school community when selecting books. Although the community may favor one viewpoint, a library must present all aspects of an issue. This is an area where consultations with professional school librarians at the school or district level are important and necessary as there may be legal and ethical issues involved.

GIFTS

Sometimes, parents or other community members may bestow gifts on the library. Most library policies stress that gifts should always be accepted and appreciated. Consult library policies and let parents know the books will be used in a manner as dictated by the gift policy, and it may be that not all gifts will be placed for student checkout. When a parent of a fifth grader wants to donate all of the books her child has outgrown, there may be a few that are not quite appropriate for the library. They may be old and shabby or slanted in viewpoint. The donator may have included some teen or adult books that are too mature for the students. Although these books may have been beloved by the giver, they may not be appropriate for the school library. Accept the books and then decide what to do. A book sale is a good idea. Even an old book is a good deal for a dime or a quarter. Offer them to teachers for personal use in their classroom libraries where they will not get as much traffic as in the library. If the items are too advanced for the school's grade level, send them to higher level schools in the district. It is wonderful to receive free items for the school library, but only keep what has a useful purpose for the collection and the students.

This Free Stuff cart is used by one of the authors to give away books and other resources not needed by the library.

WEEDING

Part of collection development is weeding. Weeding is the process of discarding books that are no longer appropriate for the collection. The term *weeding* is used because, like the flowers in a garden, the new and exciting books stand out when the old, shabby books are discarded. Materials are weeded for a variety of reasons. The most obvious reason is that they are worn and unappealing. Materials should also

FAQ
WHAT IF PARENTS FIND OUT THAT THEIR DONATIONS WERE GIVEN AWAY?

When accepting donations, let the donor know that you will use every item that you possibly can. Be truthful and tell the donor that if the books are not appropriate for your library, you will find them a good home.

Frequently Asked Questions

be weeded when they become outdated or the information presented in them is no longer accurate. Language is another reason some books are weeded. For example, when a book about airplanes mentions the "stewardess" and has pictures in black and white, it is time to remove that book and get a new more accurate title. When that book on wolves says that the grey wolf is endangered, it is giving old information that is no longer true. Because weeding takes so much time, most libraries create a weeding schedule. Each year a different part of the collection is chosen. That area is scrutinized and the collection is weeded and updated. It is understood that classics such as

This book has become moldy and needs to be weeded from the collection.

award-winning fiction and other tales that children love should not be weeded just because they were written long ago because they are timeless in their appeal. However, if the books are classics, new copies of the books are available. Instead of keeping a book that may be starting to turn yellow and smell musty, buy a new copy. A weeded collection will give students accurate answers to their questions through nonfiction books and exciting attractive new stories in fiction books.

Many people working in school libraries make excuses for not weeding. They have a problem with throwing things away, especially books, and don't want to discard items for any reason. They fear their teachers, parents, and administration will be upset and that children won't have enough materials when the weeded items are gone. Providing students with information that is inaccurate or with books that look shabby is

TIMBER CREEK HIGH SCHOOL MEDIA CENTER
FIVE-YEAR PLAN TO ADDRESS RESOURCE GAPS, 2011-2018

2011-2012	2012-2013	2014-2015	2016-2017	2017-2018
Reference	Languages (400s)	Reference	General Works (000s)	Reference
• Science Dict./Ency.	• ESOL Resources (Spanish)	• Encyclopedia	• Phenomena	• Encyclopedia (World Book)
• Sports Dict./Ency.	Health/Technology (600s)	• Almanacs	• Library/Info Sciences	• Almanac, Atlases
• Geographical Dict.	• Inventions/Inventors	• Careers	• News/Journalism	• Dictionaries
• Biographical Dict.	• Medicine, Fitness, Drugs	• Drugs, Diseases	Holiday/Folklore (390s)	Fiction – Same as 2011-2012
• Almanacs	• Engineering (Energy, Machines, Technology)	• Medical Dict./Ency.	Social Studies (300s)	Biography – Reviews
Biography – Reviews	• Travel (Air, Cars, Space Technology)	Religion (200s)	• Careers	Languages (400s)
Sciences & Math (500s)	• Nutrition	• World Religions	Languages (400s)	ESOL Resources (Spanish)
• Astronomy	Arts/Sports (700s)	• Multiculturalism	• ESOL Resources (Spanish)	Social Studies (300s)
• Math & Science Fair	• Photography	Philosophy (100s)	• Multicultural Materials	• Economics (Money, Conservation, Ecology)
• Earth & Life Sciences	• Sports (All Kinds)	• Feelings/Values	Health/Technology (600s)	• Commerce (Communications, Transportation)
• Physics	Arts/Sports (700s)	• Character Education/Ethics	• Medicine, Fitness, Drugs	Sciences & Math (500s)
• Chemistry	• Crafts	Social Studies (300s)	• Engineering (Energy, Machines, Technology)	• Astronomy
Social Studies (300s)	• Painting	• Cultural/Ethnic Backgrounds	Arts/Sports (700s)	• Math & Science Fair
• Careers	Geog. & History (900s)	• Laws	• Sports (All Kinds)	• Earth Sciences
Fiction	• Country Books	• Government	Literature (800s)	• Life Sciences
• Teachers Reading Lists	Professional	• Careers	Professional	• Physics
• Young Adult Reviews	• Principal/Teacher Input	• Commerce (Communications, Transportation)	• Principal/Teacher Input	• Chemistry
• Current Popular Titles	• Reviews	• Manners/Etiquette	• Reviews	Geog. & History (900s)
• Florida Teens Read	Fiction – Same as 2011-2012	Fiction – Same as 2011-2012	Fiction – Same as 2011-2012	• Country Books
Geog. & History (900s)	Biography – Reviews	AV – Weed same as above	AV – Weed same as above	• Native American
• Africa Books	AV – Weed same as above	Other* – As needed	Other* – As needed	History – North America
AV – Weed same as above	Other* – As needed			Other* – As Needed
Other* – As needed				

From *School Library Collection Development: Just the Basics* by Claire Gatrell Stephens and Patricia Franklin. Santa Barbara, CA: Libraries Unlimited. Copyright © 2012.

TOP TEN REASONS YOU MIGHT WANT TO WEED SOMETHING!

Sometimes it is difficult to weed a favorite book or video, but if one or more of these standards apply to the item in your hand, it is probably time to pull it from the collection.

Top 10 reasons why you should...

1. The book or AV material is torn or broken.
2. The pages of the book are yellowed or damaged.
3. The material is outdated.
4. The material contains information that is no longer true.
5. Newer, more up-to-date materials are available.
6. The subject is no longer taught at your school.
7. The material is inappropriate for your grade level.
8. The items have not circulated or are unneeded duplicates.
9. It is an encyclopedia set published five or more years ago, or other annually published material that is at least three years old.
10. The items are biased or show stereotypes.

not the answer. Teachers, parents, and others will only be upset until they see how great the library looks and how important it is for the children to have current information. Some people think if they weed, they will not have money to buy new more current materials. However, why would the principal provide money if the library shelves are packed with books and the equipment room is overflowing? Why would the principal want to invest in a dull shabby area of the school? Once the collection is weeded, there will be needs that require funding because the teachers must have current materials to support the curriculum. Some

It may feel scary to remove old books from the shelves, but weeding is important to keep the school collection inviting and current.

TOP TEN SIMPLE STEPS TO WEEDING

Top 10 reasons why you should...

Many people don't weed their collections because the idea overwhelms them. It seems like such a big task that it becomes impossible. Here are some tips to help manage the weeding process:

1. Focus on one area of the school library collection.
2. Create a list using your media management system to determine if there are any items that have never been checked out.
3. Go to the shelves and look at each item, taking books off the shelves that have never been checked out.
4. Examine each book for damage. Remove shabby, yellowed materials.
5. Check the copyright date for the age of the material.
6. Take off the shelf any inappropriate or biased items.
7. Determine if you want to promote these materials with specific groups or teachers, or if you want to delete them from your collection.
8. If discarding, process books to be discarded (see Top Ten Things to Do with Weeded Materials).
9. If you are discarding equipment, take the item off the school inventory, if applicable.
10. Decide what you will do with the discarded materials.

FAQ
ARE THERE ANY RESTRICTIONS ON HOW TO DISCARD MATERIALS?

Frequently Asked Questions

Each school district has its own policy about discarding materials. It would be bad public relations if a television station found hundreds of library books thrown away in your school's trash! The media has no idea about the professional weeding plans that school libraries follow to determine what to discard. Check your district policies. Many districts pay a vendor to pick up discarded items. Be creative. Decide what would benefit your school library the most and discard items in that manner. You could put materials on a "Free Stuff" table or have a "Friends of the Library" sale.

FAQ
CAN I GIVE MY DISCARDED BOOKS TO OTHER LIBRARIES WHO MIGHT WANT THEM?

If you have items that are too shabby or outdated for your students, why would another school benefit from them? If you are considering giving the items to a school that is lower in socioeconomic status than your school, you are just giving them more old materials, not making their school better. If you are discarding items because they are too low or too high level for your students, this might be a time to give items to your feeder schools if they are inappropriate for you, but on their level.

Frequently Asked Questions

TOP TEN WAYS TO PROCESS WEEDED MATERIALS

Weeding materials is not as simple as taking them from the shelf! It is also necessary to be sure you have removed the materials you weed from the computer system and prepare them for discarding according to your district guidelines. Below are some of the steps you may need to do:

Top 10 reasons why you should...

1. Remove book from shelves.
2. Delete the copy (or title if it is your only copy) from your media management system.
3. Keep a record of the items that you delete from your system to determine later if you will reorder the exact same thing or one on the same topic.
4. Take barcode off the weeded item.
5. Take spine label off book or AV material.
6. Take pocket out of the book.
7. Stamp "Discard" on top, bottom, and inside of book.
8. Cross out the name of your school where it was stamped inside the book.
9. Determine if you want to offer any of the weeded items to your teachers.
10. Dispose of the unwanted materials in a manner that is approved by your district.

people think it will take too much time from their other duties. Although all media personnel have some of these same feelings, it is important to weed. It should be ongoing. Use a weeding chart and make time to "clean house." If the school has not been weeded for a while, consider having a "weeding party." Invite teachers or parents or other library workers to help you. Buy a few pizzas, explain weeding criteria, and begin discarding unwanted materials. The school library will look new and vibrant, and the children will be glad that the garden was weeded.

Criteria for weeding should be found in the collection development plan. There are many sources to help decide what to weed. You may use different criteria for weeding depending on whether the material is fiction, nonfiction, or audiovisual material and equipment.

CHAPTER 3
ORDERING AND PURCHASING

BUDGETS

If the library is lucky enough to have a healthy budget or have earned some monies through a grant or book fair, the money must generally be spent within the school year. The first step in finding and spending money in an efficient manner is to learn about budgets. The principal is usually in charge of budgets at most schools. A bookkeeper usually assists the principal with tracking budget funds. Ask the principal if there is any budget money earmarked for the school library. Sometimes there may be money available, but it can only be spent in specific ways, maybe only for supplies or only for books. Find out who does the purchasing for the school library and make sure that they accept input as to what is ordered. The person working in the library with students and teachers every day will have a better idea what is needed and that input will be appreciated. If no one is assigned to purchase library resources, then the principal will probably ask library staff to oversee the purchasing.

In addition to assisting the principal with budgets, the bookkeeper usually has a hand in creating purchase orders and requisitions. Make an appointment with the bookkeeper to ask about your districts rules and policies for handling orders and other financial matters. This is essential because mishandling of budgets and financial matters can have severe consequences. It is important to work closely with whoever does the purchasing so that financial matters will be handled correctly, and the school will benefit from the efficient use of school funds.

When learning about the budget, make sure to talk to the bookkeeper often. Frequently the bookkeeper holds another position such as the school secretary so make inquiries as to who knows the most about ordering. A school secretary and bookkeeper are very knowledgeable about how the school works. Each school district and school has procedures for placing orders. Many districts will only allow orders from approved vendors. There is nothing worse than spending a large amount of time on an order only to find out that orders from that

TOP TEN FUNDING SOURCES FOR SCHOOL LIBRARIES

Top 10 reasons why you should...

There are many ways to get funding for your school library. Here are a few common funding sources that many school librarians rely on:

1. State budget funds earmarked for library materials.
2. District funds that the principal chooses to use on library materials.
3. National grants for libraries. Check the Internet for this type of grant; you'll find that many companies and foundations sponsor grants along with groups like the American Library Association.
4. Local grants may come from your city or county; there may also be local groups like the Rotary Club or Chamber of Commerce that would love to donate specific resources if you ask them.
5. PTA groups often grant funds from fundraisers to school libraries. Get to know your school's PTA parents. Donations to the library support the entire student body, and parents are often very willing to help you with grants and donations.
6. Sponsoring a book fair is a way to earn money or acquire free books based on your sales. Before agreeing to sponsor a book fair, check with your principal and bookkeeper. Be sure you understand the rules for signing contracts and handling the money generated by sales.
7. In some areas, schools help defray the cost of printing and copying by charging students a small amount for each printout. While this usually does not cover the true costs of the toner and paper, it does help and can provide a small amount of money that can support the purchase of supplies.
8. Fines for late books are controversial in school libraries but remain a common practice. Often there are rules for using fine money; for example, in some areas it can only be used to purchase new books for the school library. Be sure to consult with your school's bookkeeper on how this type of revenue can be used.
9. Local businesses are often willing to donate specific items. Identify exactly what your school needs and approach a local business to see if they are willing to help. If they cannot make a donation, they may be willing to substantially discount the price as a favor to the school.
10. Many school libraries also hold regular fundraisers. Money earned from fundraisers, such as sales of holiday or food items, might help fund purchases of materials for book clubs, new equipment, or needed supplies. Again, it is important to become familiar with your school's rules for fundraisers and how the money can be spent before agreeing to sponsor this type of event.

FAQ
HOW DO I FIND GRANTS FOR MY LIBRARY?

The Internet makes it easy to find grants available to school libraries. A recent search yielded grants such as these:

Frequently Asked Questions

Teach Award from Best Buy—http://www.bestbuy-community-relations.com/teach_awards.htm

Family Dollar Grant—http://www.dollargeneral.com/dgliteracy/Pages/family_literacy.aspx

Target Reading Grant—http://sites.target.com/site/en/company/page.jsp?contentId=WCMP04-031821

Laura Bush Foundation Grant—http://www.laurabushfoundation.org/

Improving Literacy Grants—http://www2.ed.gov/programs/lsl/index.html

These are just a few of the many grants available. Be sure to research the grants you are considering. Check their guidelines so that you know if they fund the types of projects you are proposing, and be sure you understand the application procedures and deadlines. You may also need to check with your district library staff to find out if there are any policies about writing grants that you are required to follow.

merchant are not allowed, so be sure to ask questions about this issue. The bookkeeper will know about any special forms that must be filled out when ordering. These forms are commonly called purchase order requests or requisitions. Normally specific information is needed about the order such as item numbers, specific item name, quantity, price per unit, shipping charges, and so forth. Many districts also require price quotes to be attached to the requisition request; sales people are accustomed to this procedure and will provide the quote if requested. Since libraries often order a large number of books at one time, the district may have special procedures in place for handling lengthy lists. Stay in touch with the bookkeeper throughout the ordering process, and don't be afraid to ask questions as the process continues. They also know how long the process takes. A good bookkeeper will keep trouble at bay and find money to create a library that is a true learning space.

Collections constantly need to be updated. There are so many excellent resources that need to be ordered, but it is necessary to prioritize. Using a weeding chart, note the area that has been weeded during the past year. This is probably the area to concentrate on when creating new orders. New fiction books are also a must. New materials will excite teachers and students, enhance learning, and encourage pleasure reading.

TOP TEN TIPS FOR ORDERING

Top 10 reasons why you should...

1. Make sure you know your school procedures when ordering.
2. Make sure you are using an approved vendor when you place as order.
3. Make sure you perform a collection development assessment to determine that you are not ordering items that you already have.
4. Make sure you do not pay tax (because you are a school) and that you get all the discounts and free shipping that you can negotiate.
5. Make sure you order the correct library processing when you order materials.
6. Make sure you fill the order with audiovisual items and books that are truly needed for your collection.
7. Make sure the items are chosen by you and not from a list a vendor gives you.
8. Make sure you order books that will enhance your school's curriculum.
9. Make sure you have considered suggestions from teachers and students.
10. Make sure you have a way to promote these new purchases.

FAQ
HOW DO I KNOW WHETHER TO BUY HARDBACKS OR PAPERBACKS?

Frequently Asked Questions

This is largely a matter of preference. Hardbacks, especially library bound books, last longer than paperbacks, but are much more expensive. If the item is a classic book that will become a permanent part of the collection, purchase a hardback. If you need numerous copies of a book because it is very popular at the moment, buy paperback. Soon the demand will not be as great as it is when the book is new. Picture books that are handled roughly by little ones should be hardback books. High school students would rather carry a paperback in their backpack than a heavy hardback. In general, you know your school community; use your knowledge and judgment to purchase what your students prefer.

DIGITAL MEDIA

What about digital media? What about ordering web resources or e-books? Will there come a time when there are no print materials and students learn only from the web? Perhaps, but even with all the technological advances of the past few years, that time is yet to come. However, it is important to understand that students are getting more and more information from digital media. Using the computer is the preferred research method for today's students. Although it is often faster and easier to use a handy book, students of all ages prefer using digital media, which may include their iPad or their phones. Instead of fighting this trend, we need to be aware of it and encourage students to learn how to locate the best and most accurate information from their digital media research. Many districts and schools purchase on-line databases because this is a way to make certain that the information students receive is accurate and reliable. But many schools do not have the funds for these costly services. Since it is vitally important that students become smart information consumers, be sure to ask district library staff what online services may be available to schools in the area free of charge. For instance, sometimes states will purchase databases for schools and sometimes public libraries allow schools access. Spend time exploring these services and become familiar with them. Start promoting them to students and teachers. Becoming more familiar with the strengths and weaknesses of these online products helps determine if purchasing individual subscriptions for different online databases would benefit the school.

TOP TEN TIPS FOR FINDING RELIABLE RESEARCH WEBSITES

Finding reputable websites for research is so important that many states now include media literacy standards in their curriculum requirements. School librarians are constantly teaching and encouraging students to think critically about the websites they find. Here are some of the questions they might ask a student doing Internet research:

Top 10 reasons why you should...

1. How do you know the site is reliable?
2. Who is the author of the site? What are his qualifications?
3. Why did the author create this site? What is its purpose?
4. What is the date the site was posted or updated?
5. How is the site organized and designed?
6. Are the pictures helpful or are they advertisements?
7. Do the links in the site work?
8. Does the site seem biased?
9. What is the domain of the site? Is it .gov, .edu, .org?
10. Is the information on the site better or worse than found on other sites?

FAQ
IF A DOMAIN FOR A WEBSITE IS .GOV, .EDU, OR .ORG, DOES THAT MEAN THE SITE IS RELIABLE?

Frequently Asked Questions

No matter what the URL, sites must be evaluated in order to determine their authenticity and reliability. Many .org sites are organizations with a bias or an underlying purpose. Students must be taught to double-check any site before they give credence to the information they find on its pages.

What about e-books? Will students soon be using those instead of traditional hardbacks and paperbacks? Before purchasing large numbers of e-books, it may be wise to survey students and staff. Will they be downloading books to personal devices such as a Kindle, Nook, or iPad? If so, what type of device do they have? Are e-books considered for school purchase compatible to devices available? Find out how many students have computers at home and if they have Internet access. Do the students have a personal computer, or do they share the computer with other family members? Is there a printer to enable them to print copies of book pages? The results of this survey may be surprising. Many students do not have the capacity to download all the materials they want to read, and many do not even have the funds for hand-held digital devices. Younger students still want the tactile comfort of a book read to them at bedtime. There are many considerations when planning to transition to digital technologies, and precious money should not be spent on e-books that students cannot access and use. However, school libraries recognize that e-books are the wave of the future and are incorporating them into their library collections. It is often possible to download a few free e-books and offer them to students. Many titles are available free of charge through services such as World Book Online, which you may have already purchased. Many e-books are also available on the web. Take time to explore what is offered and advertise these resources to the school community. This will also help when purchasing e-books because money will not be wasted on titles you can already access. Once you ascertain how many students use the e-books that are available, a determination can be made as to how many more should be downloaded or purchased. As digital technologies are introduced to your school, the entire community will see that the library is looking to the future.

PROCESSING AND SHELVING

It is important that library staff check with district library staff before the first orders arrive to understand the procedures required in the district and how to enter new downloads and titles into the management system. Many districts now have centralized online catalogs that allow schools to view not only their own holdings but also the collections of all the other schools as well. This type of online catalog system is called a union catalog and is very helpful for resource sharing. It also makes it vital that librarians and staff understand the way the system works along with the policies and procedures put in place by the district to manage the catalog database. Most district librarians offer periodic trainings on how to use the catalog system; attending one or more of these trainings would be an excellent idea before receiving the first order. By taking this training, you'll be prepared to handle the newly purchased resources as soon as they arrive.

Once your purchases have been delivered, they will need to be processed and shelved. When placing your order, spend the few extra dollars it costs to have the books professionally processed. Ordering processing saves you time and, in the long run, money. Vendors will ask you for processing specifications. Many times these are provided by the district. Vendors hire professional staff to correctly catalog your materials ensuring the correct placement in the library. Since the Dewey decimal system can be confusing, this is especially helpful when learning about the collection and how libraries work. Efficiently done processing keeps the collection information consistent. The order will arrive with barcodes, spine labels, and reading program information already attached in the location requested. A data download will also be sent for the computerized library management system so that books need not be manually input onto the computer. Frequently companies provide most of the processing free of charge with an order; other companies have sliding scale fees depending on the order size. If the library has a theft detection system, the system targets can be provided by the book vendor for a small fee per book. Don't let this small charge deter purchasing processing. Resources that arrive with processing already done can be out of the box and on the shelf for checkout in a matter of days. Orders without processing often remain in the back room for months waiting for staff to be trained on how to classify each item, attach pockets and barcodes, and enter them in the computer. This process is time-consuming and requires a high level of expertise.

Even with vendor-attached processing there will always be a few steps required before new materials can be checked out. There are also always new donated titles or books from a book fair or trip to the bookstore that require processing. Processing that is customary in your district should become more and more familiar through trainings and by networking with district-level contacts and the librarians at nearby schools. Items with pre-attached processing may only require someone to stamp the book with your school name and address. Some districts require books to be stamped with your school name on top, bottom, inside back cover, and inside front cover as well as on a particular page. Be consistent: for example, always stamp page 25. Books without processing require staff to create and attach Dewey decimal labels to the spine of the book. If students participate in a computerized reading program such as Accelerated Reader or Reading Counts, another spine label may be required that includes the program information. Check the books on the shelves and copy the label style to create the reading

TOP TEN STEPS FOR GETTING A BOOK "SHELF READY"

Top 10 reasons why you should...

Each school and district will have their own procedures for getting books ready to circulate. Check with your district librarian and the librarians at other schools to become familiar with what is commonly done in your area. This list is representative of what many school libraries do to prepare books for the shelves.

1. Stamp the book with your school name on the top, bottom, front, back, and on a specific page, such as page 25.
2. Place a barcode on the book, usually top left corner. Cover with a see-through label.
3. Determine what Dewey number to place on the book, usually found on the back of the title page, commonly called the verso page.
4. Place a spine label with the Dewey number on the bottom of the spine of the book. Cover with a see-through label.
5. Place a label on the spine with information for any reading program you may have purchased. Cover with a see-through label.
6. Place label on spine with a genre sticker, such as Romance, Mystery, Historical Fiction, if you wish. Cover with a see-through label.
7. Place a pocket on the page opposite the back cover. If you have a security system, tags must be placed in the book, usually under the pocket.
8. To protect book covers, place book jackets from hardback books in a cellophane sleeve and attach laminate to paperbacks.
9. Input the title into your media management system. If you must catalog the item yourself, look at the Cataloging in Publication (CIP) information usually found on the back of the title page.
10. Prominently display the book on a New Book shelf.

FAQ
WHY DO I HAVE TO STAMP MY SCHOOL NAME ON PAGE 25?

You can stamp your books wherever you wish, but students can sometimes tear out the pages you have stamped or cross-out stamps that you can see. Stamping on an inside page allows you to check if the book is yours when all other distinguishing marks are not readable.

Frequently Asked Questions

FAQ
WHAT IS A MARC RECORD?

The term MARC stands for machine access readable copy. It is a computerized format librarians use to assure that all records are uniform. It is a standard that all libraries use. Your library management software will read this record and place the text in a format that students will understand.

Frequently Asked Questions

FAQ
HOW DO I KNOW WHAT PROCESSING TO ORDER WITH MY NEW LIBRARY ITEMS?

In fact, you are not required to order any of your collection with processing. However, in order to save time and ultimately money, it is wise to get as much processing as possible with your new items. Many vendors offer free processing and shipping with your order. If you must pay for processing, it is a minimal fee for each book or audiovisual item. Of course, what processing you need depends on how you circulate your materials. Most schools use media management software. With this

Frequently Asked Questions

software, it is necessary to have a barcode and a spine label to identify where the book is located on the shelf. Many schools use a pocket in the back of the book that holds a date due card to tell students when the item is due back in the library. Most schools need their books stamped with their school name. Some schools use a sensor to prevent theft. Consult with your district librarian and look at the books on your shelves and decide what processing you will need for new items. Minimal processing is always better than too many labels or stickers.

Purchasing vendor processing helps speed up the amount of time needed to get new books on display for student checkout.

Some school libraries add labels to their books during processing to help students identify award-winning titles or books in different languages or genres. These labels can be purchased from a library supply store.

program information labels. It is important to be consistent when processing books so that patrons know what to expect and how to manage in your library. Some libraries add genre labels or award winner stickers to books to help patrons pick them out on the shelves. Each book has a barcode label affixed to the front of the book in a particular spot. Top-left corner of the front cover is the most effective position to place the barcode, especially when performing an in-ventory; but the library may have selected a different location. If that is the case, stay consistent with the existing practice to avoid confusion. Many schools place a pocket on the inside of the back cover in order to hold the date due card. Many schools also include a sensor that activates the alarm system if a book has not been checked out. Check with administration to find out if the library has a security system. If the library has a security system, become familiar with it. After materials are physically processed, the titles must be entered into the media management system so that students can access them from the electronic card catalog. Usually books that are fully processed from a vendor will have a complete MARC record so that it is only necessary to download the information to the media management system. Sometimes when a book is purchased from the neighborhood bookstore, processing is needed quickly. In that case, a title may need to be entered into your system immediately. If staff is unsure of the information necessary for a good record in the media management system, look at the help section of the software. It will explain how to enter a complete MARC record.

Once the resources are ready to be checked out, they must be made available for checkout. This could be done by a special new book display, or the books might be placed on the shelves in an orderly manner. This takes time so find help! Many schools have a library club that includes students who meet after school to work in the library. Some schools have parents who volunteer to shelve books and audiovisual items and keep them in order. Other schools invite high school students to accumulate community service hours by helping in the library.

CIRCULATION

One of the main functions of the school library is to get reading material into the hands of children. Flexible scheduling is important so that all students have access to the collection. Encourage teachers to bring their classes in whenever they are studying a topic that needs more in-depth research. Your collection can provide further insights into a topic and entice children to go beyond the classroom discussion. However, it is also very important to schedule all students into the school library so that they are able to check out books for pleasure or

There will always be some books that will require manual processing. Be sure all the steps involved in processing are fully understood before beginning to avoid time-consuming mistakes.

When ordering processing, be sure to find out if the school has a reading program such as Accelerated Reader or Reading Counts and include these labels in your processing order.

This processing form from Garrett Book Company allows the school librarian to customize the processing for a new book order.

Garrett Book Company

130 East 13th Street   PO Box 1588   Ada, OK 74821

Phone: 800-475-6884   Fax: 888-525-1560   Email: mail@garrettbooks.com   website: www.garrettbooks.com

Representative:_____ Date:_____

School District:_____

School/Library:_____

Name & Title:___Mr.___Ms._____

Address:_____

City, State, Zip:_____

Phone:__(_____)_____Fax:_____

Email Address:_____

___Fax RL ___Email RL ____Alpha Order ___Series Order

_____Reserve List or _____Ship & Bill Now

_____Books $_____

_____AR Quizzes @$2.99 ea. $_____ (Min. 20 quizzes)

Processing/Automation $_____ (Min. 10 titles)

Shipping @ $.50 per book $_____

Sales Tax (NC & CA only) $_____

APPROXIMATE TOTAL $_____

For Home Office Use Only:

AUTOMATION/PROCESSING

_____MARC Records & One Unattached Barcode $.35/bk

($15 minimum for orders of 42 books or less)

_____Fee to attach barcode $.10/bk

_____Spine Labels $.10/bk

_____Attached Spine Labels $.20/bk

(Standard Location is 1.5" from bottom of book)

_____Additional Barcode Labels $.15/bk

_____Book Pockets $.30/bk

_____Attached Pockets $.40/bk

(Includes Pocket Label w/book title & barcode number)

_____Shelf List Cards $.15/bk

_____Circulation/Date Due Cards $.15/bk

_____Date Due Slips $.10/bk _____Attached Date Due Slips $.20/bk

_____Accel. Reader Spine Labels (show Pt Value & RL only) $.10/bk

_____Attached Accelerated Reader Spine Labels $.20/bk

(Standard Location is above spine label)

_____Accelerated Reader Info Label Sets $.25/bk

_____Attached Accelerated Reader Info Label Sets $.35/bk

(Set includes Lg. Info Label & Sm. AR tag)

_____Lexile Label $.10/bk

_____Attached Lexile Labels $.20/bk

Location:_____

_____Blue Accelerated Reader Labels $.10/bk

_____Attached Blue AR Labels $.20/bk

Location:_____

_____Theft Detectors $.20/bk   _____Attached $.40/bk

Type: _____3M _____Checkpoint 9.5

LOCATIONS

AR Info Label Location:

Lg Label:_____

_____

Sm. Label:_____

_____

Pocket or Date Due Slip Location: If ordering both, specify location for each.

___Front Inside Cover ___Back Inside Cover

___Front Flyleaf   ___Back Flyleaf

Write location for additional barcode or barcode located inside the book. Be specific please.

_____

_____

_____

Circle Barcode Outside Location Below.

1	4	7	10
2	5	8	11
3	6	9	12

Back   Front

Barcode Direction:

A |||||||||||| 33557211

B 33557211

C 33557211

_____ A

_____ B

_____ C

_____**Do not cover title w/barcode**

CATALOGING OPTIONS:
* If no options are checked, standard options (indicated by ♦) will be used. Please update with each new order.*

Subject Headings:
- ♦   Sears
- ☐   Library of Congress
- ☐   Children's Library of Congress

Main Entry Letters Under Call Numbers (Excluding Bios):
- ♦   Three Letters
- ☐   Two Letters
- ☐   One Letter
  - ♦   Upper & Lower Case
  - ☐   All Caps

Fiction:
- ♦   Fic
- ☐   FIC
- ☐   F

Easy Fiction:
- ♦   E
- ☐   Treat as fiction

Easy Nonfiction:
- ♦   Treat as nonfiction
- ☐   E over Dewey Classification
- ☐   E

Biography:
- ♦   92
- ☐   B
- ☐   921

Collective Biography
- ♦   920
- ☐   Other:_____

Numbers of Letters of Biographees Surname:
- ♦   Three Letters
- ☐   Two Letters
- ☐   One Letter
- ☐   Entire name up to 12 letters

Bilingual Cataloging:

Prefix:	Classification:
♦ None	♦ Dewey
☐ SP	by subject
☐ SPA	☐ 468
☐ Sp	
☐ Spa	

Reference:
- ♦   Dewey Number
- ☐   R above Dewey
- ☐   Ref above Dewey
- ☐   REF above Dewey

Graphic Novel-Fiction:
- ♦   741.5 Dewey on all Graphic Fiction
- ☐   Follow Fiction Options
- ☐   _____above fiction options

Graphic Nonfiction
- ♦   Follow nonfiction & biography options
- ☐   _____above nonfiction & biography options
- ☐   741.5 Dewey on all graphic nonfiction & biography

AUTOMATION REQUIREMENTS:

Software System: _____   **Version:** _____

Computer Type: ____IBM Compatible ____MAC   **Delivery Type:** ____CD Rom ____Web Download ____3.5" Disk
                                                      (If no option marked, default will be Web Download)

MARC Record Format (If unsure of format, check the label on a data disk that has been successfully loaded):
____1991 USMARC Microlif/852 holding/USMARC 21   ____USMARC 949 Holdings   ____1987 USMARC Microlif

Barcode Symbology: **(For Code 39 mod 10, Code 39 mod 43 and Codabar—<u>must provide</u> 1st 13 digits of barcode)**
_____Code 3 of 9/Code 39 No Check Digit   _____Interleaved 2 of 5 Follett check digit
_____Code 3 of 9/Code 39 Mod 10 check digit   _____Codabar Mod 10 check digit
_____Code 3 of 9/Code 39 Mod 43 check digit   _____Unsure (please attach a copy of your barcode label)

Starting Barcode Number: _____
         ☐   **Please continue barcode range on file:**
            Please provide ending number of assigned range:_____

School/Library Name as it will appear on barcode labels (**maximum 30 characters**-including spaces):

— —

Location Code (Please indicate subfield for code): _____
If you have a special layout for your marc records fields, please include a copy of your special instructions.
*USMARC 949 customers MUST provide a 949 field layout sheet before records can be ordered!!

TOP TEN REASONS WHY YOU SHOULD SHELVE USING THE DEWEY DECIMAL SYSTEM

Top 10 reasons why you should...

Some schools are trying to model their school libraries on bookstores by organizing their books by genre. The trouble with this approach is that many books cross genres, and then it is difficult to decide where to put the book. Is it a romance or a mystery? Is it science fiction or action/suspense? By using the standard Dewey decimal system, your nonfiction books will be classified by genre as each numbered category represents a specific topic or subject matter. Your fiction will be easy to locate based on the F or Fic classification and then the alpha sorting based on the first three letters of the author's last name. Below are some ideas to consider when you consider re-organizing your collection.

1. The Dewey decimal system is the standard library organization system for most school and public libraries.
2. The Dewey decimal system is easy to understand.
3. The Dewey decimal system is taught on all levels so students will see a consistency from kindergarten to high school years.
4. The Dewey decimal system is constantly being updated to include new categories.
5. The Dewey decimal system uses numbers and letters that make it easy for volunteers or students to figure out how to place materials on shelves.
6. The Dewey decimal system takes the guesswork out of where to shelve an item because placement is very specific.
7. Students who learn what area of the Dewey decimal system has their favorite type of books will soon gravitate to that area of the library.
8. If you consider shelving by genre, some items fit in more than one place. Where do you shelve *Twilight*? In horror, fantasy, paranormal, romance?
9. If you consider shelving by grade level, you do not empower students to read above their level or allow them to feel comfortable reading below their grade level.
10. If you consider shelving by the point system invented by outside reading programs, students tend to read books only to earn points, not because the book looks interesting to them. This type of system does nothing to foster the love of reading.

personal growth. Today, with busy working parents and students' after-school schedules, the library may be the only chance children have of selecting and taking home a book to read. Busy parents have no time to visit the public library, and in hard economic times, they have no money to purchase books at the bookstore. The school library

FAQ
WHAT IS THE DIFFERENCE BETWEEN FIXED AND FLEXIBLE SCHEDULING?

Frequently Asked Questions

Fixed scheduling is the when classes are scheduled to visit the library media center for a specific time each week. Usually they are read a story or taught a lesson on how to handle books or find resources. Many times your principal makes this schedule and uses the library time as release time for the classroom teachers. A flexible schedule allows teachers to sign up for media center time when it most benefits their students. If they are researching the Revolutionary War, they might want to bring students in for three or four days to use books and websites to find information and type a report or create a PowerPoint to present to the class. Depending on the level you teach, you must decide what schedule is best for you. Kindergarten students may need to come in once a week to become familiar with the library and its resources. Young students may not need more than a few days to look over the materials that they check out. Upper elementary students and middle school students might need a combination of both types of scheduling. Maybe they want to come in for 15 minutes every two weeks to check out books and three or four days during times their teachers need them to find information on studied topics. In high school, students have more freedom to come to the library at various times to check out books so schedules should be flexible, leaving maximum time for students to come with classes to access books or websites for information.

collection is a boon to students who are learning to read or completing a research project.

Students need a simple routine when checking out books. They need to know simple procedures from how to look for books to where to get in line to check out books. Each library creates procedures that work for them. Some K–2 primary schools ask one student from each class to return every student's library books each morning. Those books are checked in, and each student has time each day to check out another book for that evening. Some schools have children check out books on their own. Using folders with teacher's names on them, students find their personal barcodes and scan their barcode and then scan the book's barcode to check out the book using the media management system. Whatever the procedure, make sure that all of the students know each of the steps in the check-out process. Be flexible, and change the procedure if necessary in order to make it more efficient.

It is important to periodically check circulation figures and compare them to numbers of other schools on your level. The effectiveness of the library is dependent on bringing the collection to the students. If it is

TOP TEN READING INCENTIVES TO ENCOURAGE STUDENT READERS

Top 10 reasons why you should...

There are lots of ways to encourage students to read. These are just a few that have been used by school librarians around the country.

1. Give a small piece of candy (Halloween? Valentine's Day?) for those who check out books.

2. Give a free bookmark with every book checked out.

3. Create a display with student names, and add a picture each time the child reads another book. Depending on the display, it could be a feather, a race car, a space ship, and so forth.

4. Have prizes for students who read the books for a specific contest. This could be a state reading award contest, books you have chosen on particular subjects or award-winning books such as the Newbery Award books. Start with small prizes for those who read a few books to bigger prizes for those who read all on the list.

5. Make sure reading incentives are appropriate for your level students. Small free certificates from local vendors, T-shirts, pencils, and gift cards are just a few items you can use.

6. Consider a big prize for an outstanding reader: a lunch trip to McDonald's with you in a limo for the fourth grader who reads 100 books in one year; or a $50 gift certificate for the senior who has checked out the most books in his four years of high school.

7. Put students who love particular genres in charge of a book club. The month you read a mystery have that student who has checked out all of the mystery books lead the discussion.

8. Ask students who are not your best readers to read and review books for a prize. Many media management software programs allow book reviews to be stored so all students can read them. If your system does not have that capability, check to see if your district allows students to use Amazon.com or similar sites for posting reviews.

9. Design a Battle of the Books and compete between classes or with a nearby school on your level. Give trophies for the winners.

10. Ask students what incentives they would like!

necessary to increase how many students check out books and how many books are checked out, begin promotions for different parts of the collection. Ask teachers what they are studying and create displays for materials on those topics. Create special displays for holidays or special community events. These displays will attract students and increase

Creating special displays helps draw attention to resources and capture student's interests.

Reading incentive programs help encourage children to read. This display honors students and teachers who have read all 15 titles on the state's reading list.

circulation. Consider contests to increase reading. Students love incentives and depending on the socioeconomics of the school community and the grade of the students, there are many ways to bring children to books. When they begin reading, they will find books that they love.

SHARING RESOURCES

Many districts share resources with other schools. This is beneficial because that allows one school's collection to expand to that of the entire district. Many media management systems will allow viewing of the collections of other schools in your district. Then, when searching for a particular topic, there will be multiple resources for students to use. Many states also have a union catalog that includes all school libraries in the state. Looking at a statewide database, it is easy to see if a school in another part of the state has materials you need. To borrow materials from other schools, e-mail or phone the school librarian at any school to determine if the resources you need are available.

FAQ
HOW DO I RECEIVE AND RETURN RESOURCES FROM ANOTHER SCHOOL?

Frequently Asked Questions

Many schools have a courier system that will deliver items from school to school. Many smaller districts have teachers that work at more than one school. Many times administrators go to meetings at other schools. Maybe some of your teachers live near the other schools in your district. Enlist their help. Your students and your fellow schools will be happy with this arrangement. If the school is far away, it is a little more difficult to loan and borrow materials. However, using the mail system and paying book rate to ship the book is not as expensive as you might think. When the mailman comes to your school, send the item with him. Loaning books to schools will put you in their good graces so that you can borrow from them in the future.

CHAPTER 4
MAINTAINING THE COLLECTION

REPAIR AND MAINTENANCE

Throughout the school year, the collection cannot be neglected. As new items are added to the collection, older items must be constantly evaluated. Usually this task is not difficult because teachers and students will bring worn, torn, or abused items to the attention of the library staff. Books with torn or defaced pages and broken audiovisual materials will have to be repaired or replaced. Sometimes when materials are worn out, it is an easy fix. Using book tape to fix the spine of a book or glue to secure loose pages is easy to do. But before spending time and money on supplies to repair the item, check to see if replacing the item inexpensively is an option. Considering the cost of your time as well as supplies and how long a repaired item may or may not last, sometimes replacing the damaged resource is your best course of action.

Make sure teachers and students are aware that their help is needed in evaluating the collection. Ask them to alert staff if an item is in need of repair. While library club members or volunteers shelve books, they can help look for copies in need of extra care and make basic repairs. Students who stay after school can provide significant help by performing simple repair tasks such as replacing barcode protectors or re-taping book covers that are falling off. To help prevent damage, teach little ones how to care for library books to minimize damage to the collection. Children who help in the school library develop a sense of ownership with regards to the facility and its collection. This sense of pride pays dividends as student helpers expand their knowledge and begin to teach their peers about library use, policies, and procedures.

Teachers and students can also help maintain an outstanding collection by making suggestions for new items to purchase. Children who frequent bookstores and public libraries will have ideas for what to buy. This will make sure resources appeal to all of the students. Even the students who are not enthusiastic readers will ask for things that

Before repairing a damaged book such as this one, decide if the repair is worth the time and effort. Many times it is better to replace the item with a new copy.

interest them such as a novelization of a current movie, video game, or TV show. Pay attention to requests from this type of student; the less-than-enthusiastic readers are the ones you especially want to try to hook with something they will enjoy reading.

Some schools have grant-writing committees that include teachers and parents who will write grants to provide resources needed to keep the library collection up-to-date. Other schools have programs that will increase the collection and give parents and students a chance to help the school. These programs might enlist parents to donate a book to the library on their child's birthday or to honor their graduation. Donation programs like this increase the collection and leave students with a good feeling about their school.

INVENTORY THE COLLECTION

An annual inventory is an important part of maintaining the collection. An inventory lets you know the state of the collection and provides information and data to let the administration and community know if the collection is meeting the needs of the students. Undertaking an inventory is not difficult with today's computer management systems for libraries.

Before starting the inventory, consult with the district librarian and other library contacts in the area to learn if there are any inventory procedures particular to the local district. For example, some school boards require each school library to submit an annual report of the inventory data. Find out about any district level requirements before beginning in order to plan accordingly. Develop a strategic plan as to when to begin the inventory and when it will be done. There is no need to close the library when inventorying the collection. In fact, if items continue to circulate while the inventory is going on, there is less physical work to do. The software knows what items are circulating and marks those as found. Then you scan all of the items on the shelves and download the scans into the media management system. Enlist

FAQ
IF EVERY PURCHASE IS SUPPOSED TO HAVE RATIONALE BEHIND IT, WHY SHOULD WE BUY A BOOK RECOMMENDED BY A STUDENT?

If a student requests a book, you can be sure that he will read it. Why buy books that no one will read? One of the first rules of working in a library is customer service: getting children what they want is good customer service. Once they have read that book that you bought especially for them, they will venture out to books that you recommend to them. They will also tell their friends about the book so that it will circulate over and over.

Frequently Asked Questions

This does not mean that we purchase every title requested by a student. It is a good idea to quickly check the books students request before buying them. Before going to the bookstore you can search for student requests on the Internet; check the title for a quick summary and reviews. At the bookstore, take a few minutes to scan the cover and read a few pages from the book. Are there any reviews printed on the cover that help you know what the book is about? Most books requested by elementary school students are probably relatively safe for purchase. As students age, however, some books may contain mature scenes or language that may not be appropriate for your school level. Students have a right to read what they want, but keep in mind that your school library should reflect community standards, so taking a few minutes to preview a book request before purchasing it is important.

the help of volunteers, after-school library club, or a few devoted students to accomplish the task. Look for a tutorial on the media management's software's website to explain the details of the program or sign up to attend training at the district office. Inventory can take as long as necessary. Starting the inventory in January and ending in May allows time to scan and upload when time allows. It also allows time to teach students how to help and to allow them time to do a little each day. The rest of the school will be unaware that an inventory is taking place.

Once the inventory is over, look at the data to see how it will influence purchases in the future. Undoubtedly the inventory will help with weeding as dog-eared and shabby books are found. It will also help by identifying lost books so that they can be deleted from the catalog. It is very frustrating for students to look for books that are no longer available. Deciding whether these items need to be replaced or not is easy after looking at circulation figures and copyright dates of lost items. Possibly the lost item does not need to be replaced, but it might be necessary to purchase a newer book on the same topic.

Taking inventory is easier than ever. Most library management software uses portable devices to scan the library holdings on the shelves. The scans are then downloaded into the management software to account for each inventoried item.

After the inventory is complete, share the data with the administration and district library personnel. They will want to know how many books and other resources are available and how many are missing. Don't look at this as a negative, but as a way to make the administration aware of the needs of the library. If the data is complete, there may be a good case for more funding. If a weak area has been identified, the administration may know of grants that can help. Principals also often have money in their budget that they need to use or return if it is not spent. Inventory findings often justify spending this type of funding on the school library. Use the data as an advantage to

TOP TEN STEPS IN AN INVENTORY

Top 10 reasons why you should...

While each brand of library automation software will do the inventory in a slightly different way, the basics of the process are all the same. Here is a quick list of steps to help you get started.

1. Consult your district library staff for any inventory requirements in your district.
2. Attend inventory training or review the steps and software guidelines for your computer system.
3. Create a plan for tackling the process. Be sure to include all scanable items in your database.
4. Print a shelf list and put shelves in Dewey decimal order.
5. Charge your scanners and train your volunteers to use them.
6. Physically scan each book, audiovisual material or other resource and download the scans into the media management system.
7. When all have been downloaded, print a list of the unscanned items.
8. Physically look for those items on the shelves and scan those that are found.
9. Print or save a list of lost items.
10. Delete items that have been missing on multiple inventories. Generally this is done if an item has been missing for two years; however, district policies vary so it is important to consult your district librarian before doing this.

FAQ
IF I REALIZE SOMETHING IS MISSING DURING MY INVENTORY, SHOULD I REPLACE IT?

It depends on the item. If the item is checked out frequently, that means there is a demand for the item and you may want to go ahead and replace any missing copies. For a well-loved fiction book, replace it if it is still checked out frequently and you know your new copy will be used. If it is a nonfiction book that directly supports curriculum, it may be checked out frequently because teachers need information on that topic to support their classes. With nonfiction books, you may want to ask yourself if they need that actual book or AV material that you are missing, or do they just need the information it contains? It is probably a good idea to update an older nonfiction item with a newer edition or title on the same topic. The information will be more current and more accurate. Unless the older item is unique in some way, the teachers and students will appreciate more current information.

Frequently Asked Questions

let the administration understand that the library staff wants to make the school library a vibrant, exciting place for students to work and learn.

At the end of the school year, with the inventory complete, it is time to begin the process of collection development all over again. Look at this as an exciting part of working in the library. By thinking about and creating a plan for the new year, the needs of teachers and students will be fulfilled and your school will be a better place to learn.

CONCLUSION

Hopefully after reading this book, you feel comfortable asking for help from district librarians in selecting, ordering, processing, and marketing materials for your library. Working in a school library is a busy and ever-changing job. Understanding your district's policies and procedures is important. Staying organized and sticking to the procedures you create are also essential in making collection development easier. At the same time, you must develop an attitude of flexibility that will allow you to adjust your approach to collection development as needed so that your library keeps pace with changes in curriculum, new media and technologies, and school policies.

The school library is the heart of any school. Children of all ages see the library as a place that enriches their learning and provides a stimulating environment and exciting resources. It is the place that provides equity for needy students and challenging materials for advanced students. When a student finds just the right resource to complete his project or "the best book he ever read," you know that you have selected materials that make a difference in a child's achievement.

The school library is only as good as its collection. The information provided in this book is meant to help with practical tips to build and improve the collection. Spending taxpayer money is a huge responsibility, but if you seek the help of your district librarian, give informed input, and follow simple guidelines, you will spend funds wisely and develop a collection that teachers and students alike will use and enjoy. Good luck and enjoy working in an outstanding school library with a great collection!

INDEX

ABOUT THE AUTHORS

CLAIRE GATRELL STEPHENS is a National Board Certified Teacher who is the library media specialist at Freedom High School in Orlando, Florida. Claire received her MFA from Southern Methodist University in Dallas, Texas and is currently finishing her Education Specialist degree in Educational Leadership at Nova Southeastern University. She is the author of *Coretta Scott King Award Books: Using Great Literature with Children and Young Adults, Picture This!: Using Picture Story Books for Character Education in the Classroom*, and co-author of *Library 101: A Handbook for the School Library Media Specialist*.

PATRICIA FRANKLIN is the library media specialist at Timber Creek High School in Orlando, Florida. She has a Masters in educational media and is a National Board Certified Teacher. She is the co-author of *Library 101: A Handbook for the School Library Media Specialist*.

Edwards Brothers Malloy
Thorofare, NJ USA
October 15, 2013

MAR 1 3 2014